THE HIDDEN HEROES OF THE GOSPELS

THE HIDDEN HEROES OF THE GOSPELS

Female Counterparts of Jesus

Joseph A. Grassi

THE LITURGICAL PRESS
COLLEGEVILLE, MINNESOTA

Cover: Woodcut by Robert F. McGovern. Design by Don Bruno.

Library of Congress Cataloging-in-Publication Data

Grassi, Joseph A.

The hidden heroes of the Gospels.

Bibliography: p.

1. Women in the Bible. 2. Bible. N.T. Gospels—
Criticism, interpretation, etc. I. Title.

BS2555.2.G678   1989   226'.0922'088042   88-27182

ISBN 0-8146-1591-0

To my own dear counterparts,
Carolyn, Eddie, and Peter

CONTENTS

INTRODUCTION

The word "hidden" in the title of this book has special significance. First of all, the four Gospels were not public documents but secret books. They were written for small "in groups" that could understand these writings because their members possessed a secret key to their meaning. This key was their own unique relationship to the characters in the Gospels, especially the hero, Jesus. They called this relationship faith or trust. However, it was not faith in a person of the past but in one they considered very much alive. They were keenly aware of his presence not only in their daily lives but in their community meetings for prayer, worship, and mutual encouragement.

Moreover, the word "hidden" is apropos because the Gospels were actually books of secrets whose meaning gradually unfolded to their audience during a "live performance." By this I mean that the Gospels were not meant to be read silently by anyone except on rare occasions. They were composed to be read aloud by a skilled reader. The Gospels were a live performance like a stage play or an opera. Today we go to such performances for entertainment or for personal enrichment. We look forward to possible new insights and experiences. This was true in ancient times as well. People listened to the Gospels as live performances. They also believed that active listening would bring them new energy to transform their lives and deepen their relationship to God as well as to one another. Each time they listened, they anticipated the discovery of new secrets in the Gospel drama that would deeply move them.

Every performance of a drama contains such secrets; they are gradually revealed to the audience in an expanding cre-

scendo. The suspense is sustained through hints, foreshadow-
ings, careful repetition, special cues, surprises, and powerful
images. One of the exciting results of modern biblical research
is the rediscovery of the Gospels as narrative drama.[1] They follow a carefully planned plot leading to a definite conclusion
through a gradual progression of events. They have consistent characters who each play a special role in bringing out the
full emotional impact of the story. They usually have heroes
who are the centers of the drama. The author skillfully presents
the story to the audience so that they can identify with the
characters and become deeply involved with them. The drama
is meant to be understood as a whole, with each scene, actor,
and dialogue contributing toward its total effect and planned
climax.

In all four Gospels the supreme hero is Jesus. All the events
and discourses lead to his heroic death and its meaning for
the characters/audience. As a result, each part of the drama
must be interpreted in light of this climactic scene and conclusion. This is similar to the separate parts of an opera, play, or
movie; they cannot be interpreted piecemeal but must be understood in light of the total plot, especially its climax.

As a counterpart to the hero Jesus, we find in the Gospels
a portrait of the ideal disciple who follows Jesus' way even as
far as the cross. The story of Jesus' life and death is told in
such a way that the disciples/audience can identify with it. As
they do so, they can share the hope that their lives, and even
their suffering and death, can also be heroic and affect others
as Jesus' did.

One of the great surprises in listening to the Gospels is the
discovery that the ideal disciple is often portrayed as a woman.
This is especially striking when we remember that the Gospels
were written in a patriarchal society in which male roles were
dominant.[2] In such a setting it would be expected that women
would remain hidden in the background. Yet the rediscovery
of the Gospels as dramatic narrative can lead us to insights
that previously eluded us. This is especially true of the secret

heroes of the Gospels. Their hidden role emerges gradually until the full impact suddenly hits the audience at the end.

In writing this book, I have reviewed the contributions of many biblical scholars and have made use of them throughout. For easier reading, I have usually avoided mentioning authors' names in the text; instead, I have used footnotes so that the reader can refer to the appropriate sources for more detailed information on many of the points made in the book. Also included at the end is a bibliography of the sources consulted in writing this book.

My hope is that readers may discover for themselves these hidden models of discipleship and appreciate the unique contribution they make to understanding the four Gospels. Then they will grasp the full impact of Jesus' statement about the woman who anointed his head at Bethany: ''And truly, I say to you, wherever the gospel is preached in the whole world, what she has done will be told in memory of her'' (Mark 14:9; Matthew 26:13). These words are not just an accessory to the Gospel but an essential part of it.

CHAPTER ONE

THE GOSPEL OF MARK

Her "whole life" for the "whole world" (12:44; 14:9)

Mark's Audience

For a realistic understanding of the Gospel of Mark, we need a good picture of his audience. The same is true of an opera composed, for example, by Verdi. If we understand the sharp liberation struggle that was going on in Italy during his time, we can better appreciate the underlying themes of some of his arias. We can also realize why they aroused such excitement and contagious enthusiasm in his audiences.

In regard to audiences, we should distinguish between what is often called "the ideal or implicit audience" and the "actual audience" of a Gospel.[3] An ideal audience, sometimes called an "implied audience" is an imagined group of people to whom the author addresses the Gospel. With them in mind, the author plans an ideal response for them to make to the dramatic narrative. An actual audience is made up of the actual people who would be likely to be listening to the Gospel at some historical period, whether two thousand years ago or today. First, let us look at the actual historical audience at the time Mark's Gospel was written.

The Actual Historical Audience of Mark's Gospel

The best clues to this audience are found within the Gospel document itself. The very first words tell us that it is a "confessional document," that is, one written for people believing that a certain Jesus is the promised Christ or Messiah. Mark writes, "The beginning of the gospel of Jesus Christ, ['the Son of God' is added in some manuscripts]" (1:1).

In general, it can be safely assumed that the Gospel addresses primarily Gentile Christians, not Jewish Christians, because Mark has to explain Jewish customs and beliefs to them. For example, in regard to foods, the author makes the following aside: "For the Pharisees, and all the Jews, do not eat unless they wash their hands" (7:3). For other examples, see 12:18; 14:12; 15:42. The writer also has to translate into Greek the Aramaic words and phrases that were originally used. Thus, when Jesus raises up the daughter of Jairus, he says, "Talitha cumi." Mark immediately adds, "which means, 'Little girl, I say to you, arise'" (5:41). For other examples, see 3:17; 7:11, 34; 15:22, 34.

Most important, however, are the many indications that the audience lived in a time of intense crisis due to heavy persecution on account of their faith. At times they even faced death for what they believed in. Following are some of the Gospel texts pointing to this atmosphere of crisis and persecution. First we have texts containing linguistic reference to persecution, and second, those that are best understood in this light.[4]

The texts with specific references to suffering and persecution include the parable of the seed, which describes those who "have no root in themselves, but endure for a while; then, when tribulation or *persecution* arises on account of the word, immediately they fall away" (4:17). When Peter inquires about the fate of those who leave all things and follow him, Jesus replies that they will receive a hundred-fold reward along with *persecutions* (10:30). James and John ask Jesus for the first places at his right and left hand in the kingdom. Jesus replies that they will drink his cup of suffering and be baptized with the same baptism he is to undergo (10:39). Finally, in Jesus' last discourse on the Mount of Olives there are specific predictions of hatred, being delivered up to trial before governors and kings, and betrayal by family members (13:9-13). This persecution comes from fellow Gentiles, since it is explicitly stated that it will be a witness to them, followed by a preaching of the gospel to all the world (13:10).

A second group of texts includes those that are best understood against the background of an oppressed and persecuted community. Among them are the story of the storm at sea with Jesus asleep as the disciples face the danger of death (4:35-41); Jesus' call to take up the cross and follow him, even to the extent of being willing to lose life itself in order to save it; the consequences of shame to confess Jesus when the Son of Man returns (8:34-38).

The specific time of this persecution probably began under the Roman emperor Nero during the sixties and continued during the Jewish War with Rome from 66 to 70 A.D.[5] The Romans were unable to distinguish between Christians and revolting Jews, especially since Jesus was a Jew and had been crucified as a suspected revolutionary under the Roman governor Pontius Pilate. The severe persecution brought unbelievable turmoil to Christian communities. There was division within families as some converts were accused by "patriotic" brothers, sisters, or even parents to Roman authorities and were abandoned by former friends (13:12). Believers could well identify with Jesus' words on the cross, "My God, my God, why have you forsaken me?" (15:34).

Another connected crisis for the Markan community was the destruction of the Jewish Temple in 70 A.D., which had probably occurred by the time Mark's Gospel was written. This was considered a great, significant act of God, since Christians believed that God was behind the events of history. Consequently, some Christian prophets were teaching that this was a sign of the end of the world and of the imminent return of Jesus in power. In his last discourse Jesus warned against these views: "Then if any one says to you, 'Look, here is the Christ!' or 'Look, there he is!' do not believe it" (13:21). To support their words, these prophets performed signs and wonders. Mark quotes Jesus as predicting that this would happen:

". . . false prophets will arise and show signs and wonders, to lead astray, if possible, the elect" (13:22).

A belief in a speedy return of Jesus in power to vindicate their suffering would have been an immense though deceptive consolation for Christians under intense pressure. It would have led them to value miracles and power as the weapons of "superstar" Christians to face the abusive forces of imperial Rome. In his final discourse Jesus warned the community against such views and told them that the destruction of Jerusalem was not a sign of his imminent return. In fact, that time is known by no one at all, not even the Son of Man: "But of that day or hour no one knows, not even the angels in heaven, nor the Son, but only the Father" (13:32).

The Ideal Disciple in Mark's Gospel

In response to these problems, Mark presents to his audience the image of an ideal disciple modeled on Jesus, especially his heroic death and its results. Mark wants to assure his audience about the effects and meaning of their own suffering and possible death. Will it be all in vain? Or is there something definite in God's plan to provide them comfort? This is especially needed, since they have been told not to accept the predictions of some teachers and prophets that Jesus is about to return in power to vindicate them by a triumphant victory over their Roman adversaries and persecutors.

Mark adopts a dramatic narrative to get his message across to his audience. This type of presentation has the following characteristics: "the study of narrative emphasizes the unity of the final text . . . the narrator's point of view in telling the story is consistent throughout. The plot is coherent; events that are anticipated come to pass; conflicts are resolved; predictions are fulfilled. The characters are consistent from one scene to the next, fulfilling the roles they take on and the tasks they adopt."[6]

In view of this structure and form of dramatic narrative, we cannot follow Mark's message through the usual rules of logic.

"Proofs" are simply not presented in that way. Instead, the laws of rhetoric and oral persuasion must be applied. These laws rely on repetition, comparisons, contrast, and the total effect of the dramatic plot. This total effect unfolds through a gradually expanding crescendo, ending in a climax. This ending reveals the meaning of all the individual scenes and dialogue leading up to it.

Here we will follow a valuable schema proposed by V. K. Robbins showing the dramatic sequence for the expanding dynamics of Mark's Gospel.[7] In this schema the teacher/disciple sequence is considered the core of the Gospel narrative drama.

The Initial Sequence: Summons and Response (Mark 1:1–3:6)

The first words of Jesus to his disciples really summarize and outline the whole message of Mark. Jesus calls Andrew, Peter, James, and John as his first disciples and tells them, "Follow me and I will make you become fishers of human beings" (1:17). This means that if they follow him as far as the cross, they can cast out their own nets to bring other people into the kingdom just as Jesus did. This general summons already announces the results of following Jesus even in persecution and death. The rest of the Gospel will fill in the details. In writing this, Mark presents Jesus as practicing what he preaches. Jesus' own preaching begins under the shadow of a threat to his own life. John the Baptist, his predecessor, has just been arrested (1:14) and is awaiting death for daring to be a prophet. Despite this, Jesus goes ahead on a path leading in the same direction.

In ancient rhetorical procedure, the opening of a drama is linked to the beginning and end to highlight its primary message. In the beginning, Jesus receives a decisive revelation at his baptism. The heavens open and God tells him, "You are my beloved Son" (1:11). This voice seems to come privately to Jesus, for in Mark's Gospel no one knows who he really is. The word "Son" has a strong nuance of dedicated obedience, especially in light of all that follows in the Gospel.

The end of Jesus' life in the Gospel drama is also linked to the beginning in this way: again a dramatic opening (the tearing of the Temple veil) takes place following his death (15:38). The same Greek verb for "tear" (*schizō*) is used in both stories. The centurion, deeply impressed by the way that Jesus died, exclaimed, "Truly this man was the Son of God!" (15:39). Since Mark has been emphasizing Jesus' faithful fulfillment of God's plan in the Scriptures, the sense of the word "Son" is closely connected with obedience. Throughout the Gospel no human being besides the centurion ever proclaims Jesus as Son in this manner. Only his obedience unto death reveals him as a faithful Son of God.

The middle part of the Gospel is likewise linked with its beginning and end. Again a voice from heaven is heard at Jesus' transfiguration. However, this time the voice is addressed not to Jesus but to his disciples: "This is my beloved Son; listen to him" (9:7). We recall the mention of "Son" at Jesus' baptism and in the centurion's words at his death. In the beginning and the end, Jesus is a faithful Son, obedient to God's word, even if it means death. In the middle part, however, it is the disciples who are asked to obey Jesus' difficult teaching: "Those who wish to follow me must deny themselves, take up their cross and follow me; those who would save their lives will lose them" (8:34). Consequently, the way of the audience/disciple, like that of Jesus, is obedience. However, it is obedience to God's voice through Jesus. We will see later that obedience is the key to the meaning of Jesus' death as well as to that of the ideal disciple.

The Intermediate Phase in the Teacher/Disciple Cycle: Teaching and Learning (Mark 3:7–12:44)

For discovering Mark's portrait of the ideal disciple, the central section of his Gospel is most important. This begins with Jesus' question, "Who do you say that I am?" and Peter's answer, "You are the Messiah" (8:29).[8] Jesus then orders Peter to be silent and begins to explain this title through three predictions about his coming sufferings and death. Each prediction in turn is followed by teachings on the nature of the ideal disciple who follows Jesus' way of the cross (8:31–12:45). "He began to teach them that the Son of man must suffer many things, and be rejected by the elders and the chief priests and the scribes, and be killed, and after three days rise again. And he said this plainly. And Peter took him, and began to rebuke him. But turning and seeing his disciples, he rebuked Peter, and said, 'Get behind me, Satan! For you are not on the side of God, but of human beings' " (8:31).

The word "must" in 8:31 implies a necessity based on God's plan in the Scriptures. Only conformity to such a plan could make the coming tragedy meaningful instead of a tragic waste. Peter is shocked by the very idea and rebukes Jesus. Jesus calls him a "Satan" because he regards the temptation as diabolical. Later, in his dying moments, Jesus will face the same temptation as bystanders and Jewish leaders tempt him to come down from the cross and prove that he is the Messiah by a great act of power (15:29-32).

The teaching on discipleship (8:34-36) follows the same sequence as Jesus' own way: those who wish to follow him must suffer (take up the cross) and be willing to die (lose their life for his sake). However, Jesus does not promise his disciples that they will immediately rise again. Instead, he focuses on a coming judgment at the return of the Son of Man: "Whoever is ashamed of me and of my words in this adulterous and sinful generation, of that person will the Son of man also be ashamed, when he comes in the glory of his Father with the holy angels" (8:38).

Thus the sequence for the disciple is suffering, death, parousia (the return of Jesus). We draw attention to this difference because it will play an important part later. It will be seen that only the suffering and death of the disciple will make possible Jesus' return, which will be a worldwide event. Jesus' words on discipleship are so difficult that a voice from God at Jesus' transfiguration must enjoin the disciples to obey them: "Listen to him" (9:7). Only absolute faith will enable the disciple/audience to follow Jesus' impossible teaching.

This type of faith is illustrated by the cure of the "impossible case" of the epileptic boy (9:14-29). His frightful seizures gave him the appearance of death: ". . . the boy was like a corpse; so that most of them said, 'He is dead' " (9:26). Yet Jesus took him by the hand and raised him up. This death-to-life theme is directed to an audience facing the prospect of excruciating sufferings and even death. Jesus' words to the boy's doubting father convey a message to an audience in time of severe crisis: "All things are possible to the one who believes" (9:23).

The second prediction and the sequence of cross and discipleship (9:31-10:31) confirm the first. However, there is a typical dramatic expansion. The element of betrayal is added: "The Son of man will be delivered into the hands of men, and they will kill him; and when he is killed, after three days he will rise" (9:31). Following this are teachings that reflect the theology of the cross as the community is confronted with abusive Roman power.[9] On the road the disciples argue as to who is the greatest. To reverse expectations of human power, Jesus places a child in their midst as a teaching illustration and announces, "If any one would be first, he/she must be last of all and servant of all" (9:35).

The disciples also want to use coercive power to keep someone not of the Twelve from exorcising demons in the name of Jesus. Jesus will not allow this and answers, "Do not forbid him; for no one who does a mighty work in my name will be able soon after to speak evil of me. For one who is not against us is for us" (9:39-40). It is interesting that Jesus' teaching on divorce occurs in the same context of the use of external power over others: a husband has no right to divorce a wife by giving her a written notice of dismissal (10:2-9). Also, little children are not to be dismissed as an act of power by the disciples. Jesus receives them and embraces them as a sign of their priority in the kingdom (10:13-16).

The difficult sayings of Jesus about power and the cross
have special application to money and material wealth. A rich
young man comes up to Jesus and asks to be a follower. Jesus
looks at him, loves him, and replies, "You lack one thing; go,
sell what you have, and give to the poor, and you will have
treasure in heaven; and come, follow me" (10:21). At the end
of the second section, Peter asks what those persons will have
who leave all things and follow Jesus. Jesus replies that those
who are forced to leave family or possessions and who undergo
persecution will have eternal life in the age to come (10:28-31).
Once again the sequence is persecution, suffering, and parousia (seemingly indicated by "the age to come").

The third cross-and-discipleship section (10:32-45) becomes
even more explicit. Jesus will be delivered up to the Gentiles,
who will mock him, spit upon him, and crucify him (10:33-34).
Here we have the first reference to the Romans and the actual
events of crucifixion. This prepares the way for the story of
James and John, who ask to have a special place at Jesus' right
and left hand in his glory in the coming kingdom (10:35-45).
Jesus replies that they do not realize what they are asking for.
To be with him, they must share his cup and be plunged into
the same baptism of suffering and death that he will undergo.
Once again we have the sequence of suffering, death, and
parousia.

We note that the third element is the parousia because of
the use of the word "glory" by the two disciples. The same
word is used of the coming kingdom and the return of Jesus
here and in Jesus' first prediction (8:38). The story of James
and John brings out the necessary link between suffering and
parousia. The two brothers must undergo suffering and even
death in order to take part in Jesus' return. Only a close union
with Jesus and a voluntary share of his cup of suffering and
death will assure them of a place in the coming "glory." The
closing statement emphasizes this union with Jesus: "The Son
of man came not to be served but to serve, and to give his life
as a ransom for many" (10:45).

So far we have noted the sequence of suffering, death, and the return of Jesus in the three discipleship sections. Yet we have seen no explicit causal link between suffering or death and this return of Jesus, which is presumably a worldwide phenomenon (this will become more evident in later texts). We have a strong hint of a causal relationship in Jesus' statement that the Son of man has come to "give his life as a ransom for many" (10:45). The predicted death of the sons of Zebedee is in imitation of this. Therefore, it seems that their persecution and death would be a sacrifice or offering like that of Jesus. Thus it would be connected to, and even the cause of, the return of Jesus in triumph. However, the links are not strong enough to make a definite case. We must rely on Mark's dramatic narrative to disclose closer connections as the plot goes into its final stages.

Connections between Jesus' death and the world start to become stronger as Jesus enters Jerusalem for the last time. Mark makes a strong link between the Temple cleansing and Jesus' death by noting that this incident resulted in immediate plans by the chief priests and scribes to destroy Jesus (11:18). The author also draws special attention to Jesus' statement about the future meaning of the Temple: "Is it not written, 'My house shall be called a house of prayer for all the nations'? But you have made it a den of robbers" (11:17).

The parable of the vinedressers (12:1-12) also connects Jesus' death and the world. The vinedressers send away the servants of the owner; finally they even kill the beloved son of the owner and cast him out of the vineyard. As a result, Jesus announces that the owner will return, punish the evil vinedressers, and give the vineyard to others (12:9). This implies that the exclusive place of Israel is at an end and that others (the rest of the world) will have the vineyard of the kingdom of God.

Only in the last part of the Gospel do we find very specific indications that the persecution or death of the disciple, like that of Jesus, will cause the preaching of the gospel in the whole world, and thus prepare the way for the return of Jesus. The greatest comfort of the disciple/audience will be to know that their sufferings are not in vain but will have a startling worldwide effect.

The Final Phase of the Teacher/Disciple Relationship: Farewell and Death (Mark 13:1–16:8)

Jesus' farewell address and last testament to his disciples takes place on the Mount of Olives just before the passion story. It constitutes an important key to the Gospel of Mark. The tone and introduction for Jesus' last words are set by the story of the poor widow. In contrast to the large offerings of the rich, she gave "everything she had, her whole living" (12:44). Later we will see the importance of this story as part of Mark's gradual disclosure of the secret hero of the Gospel. The widow's offering is meant to be a model for the ideal disciple in Jesus' last discourse; such a disciple is willing to give even his or her life in imitation of the Master. At the end of the discourse we find the plot in motion to put Jesus to death. The scribes and chief priests plan how to arrest Jesus secretly before the Passover (14:1-2).

What will be the results of this symbolic life-offering of the widow? Mark has Jesus predict this for the community as the Gospel broadens the ideal disciple's portrait that has been presented thus far. First of all, the disciples will continue and duplicate the fate of their Master: "They will deliver you up to councils; and you will be beaten in synagogues; and you will stand before governors and kings for my sake, to bear testimony before them [*eis martyrion autois*]" (13:9).

Later this parallel will be brought out in detail. Jesus will be brought before the council (14:55), where he will openly confess who he is before the high priest (14:62) and be found deserving of death. Following this, he will be beaten and struck as the disciple will be (13:9). Then he will be brought before the governor Pilate, like the audience arraigned before governors in 13:9. Thus Jesus' witness to the Gentiles, leading to his death, will be duplicated by his disciples. The last discourse specifically mentions that the suffering and persecution of the disciples/audience are linked to a witness to the Gentiles (13:9) and to the preaching of the gospel to the Gentile world: "the gospel must first be preached to all nations" (13:10).

To stress the importance of the above statements, Jesus repeats them with more detail. "When they bring you to trial and deliver you up, do not be anxious beforehand what you are to say" (13:11). The Holy Spirit will answer for them (13:11). This shows that the disciples' trial is really the continuation of Jesus' own. The general "delivering up" of 13:9 is now specified. Brothers will report brothers and children will report parents to the Roman authorities (13:12). Thus there will be new "Judases" like the "brother" of Jesus who betrayed him to the authorities.

This betrayal of the audience/disciple may lead to death, as in the case of Jesus. Mark mentions the possible death of the disciple for the first time in 13:12: "Brother will deliver up brother to *death*." How the disciple dies will be of supreme importance: "The one who endures to the end will be saved" (13:13). Here we have a specific reference to the *manner* of death. This will be the special focus of Mark's later description of Jesus' death, which so impressed the centurion and caused his confession that Jesus was Son of God (15:39).

From the above, we find a valuable indication that the suffering and even death of the persecuted disciple are intimately connected with a testimony or *martyrion* to the Gentiles that will bring about the preaching of the gospel in the whole world. This counteracts the false prophets who proclaimed that Jesus was already beginning to return with power to vindicate his suffering community. Jesus had predicted that these prophets would make statements such as "Look, here is the Christ!" or "Look, there he is!" and lead many people astray (13:21-22). In contrast, persecuted Christians are not to look for miracles to save them from their oppressors nor await an imminent vindicating return of Jesus in power. Instead, Jesus announces that the real heralds of his return will be the persecution, suffering, and even death of his disciples. This will occasion a witness to the Gentiles and the worldwide preaching of the gospel (13:9-10).

To sum up, Jesus states that his return cannot take place until the gospel is preached to the whole world. This in turn will be made possible by a testimony or *martyrion* of the persecution, suffering, and even death of the disciples/audience. Therefore, the destruction of Jerusalem by the Romans is not a cosmic act of God preceding Jesus' imminent return; it is instead a local act of God predicted by Jesus. The final return will be characterized by a universal call to the elect from the ends of the earth (13:24-27). This means that there will be such ''elected ones'' all over the world. It implies also that a worldwide preaching of the gospel will make this a real possibility (13:10).

As a result, the necessary sequence in God's plan is (1) the suffering, persecution, and possible death of the disciple; (2) the resulting testimony or *martyrion* to the world; (3) the return of Jesus in triumph. The time sequence for all this is unknown. It is a secret known only to the Father; not even the Son knows it (13:32).

The Master's farewell address is sealed by a covenant meal between Jesus and his disciples that is continued by Mark's audience. The breaking and eating of bread take on special meaning as a means of identification with the Master. This is especially true of the cup signifying a share in his death. Jesus describes it as ''my blood of the covenant, which is poured out for many'' (14:24). This illustrates the previous statement of Jesus to James and John that they must drink his cup in order to share his glory (10:35-40). The results of the shared cup of suffering and even death are also predicted with the words ''poured out for many.'' This hints that Jesus' death will bring benefits to others and that the disciples' similar fate will do the same. This imitation of Jesus is also found in the concluding verse of the story of James and John. Jesus says, ''The Son of man also came not to be served but to serve, and to give his life as a ransom for many" (10:45).

Following the Last Supper are the narratives of Jesus' agonizing prayer before his arrest, his trial and confession before the high priest and Pilate, and finally the way of the cross. These were already predicted in general terms in Jesus' last discourse and are now carried out in action. There is no need to go into them in detail here. Mark knows that his audience can identify with every moment of the drama as they face their own arrest, trial, and possible death. The author wants them to be confident that Jesus went through the whole process himself and was able to go ahead only after an agonizing decision made possible by his persevering prayer at Gethsemane.

We must, however, give very special attention to the concluding death scene of Jesus and its effects. The whole Gospel has been moving toward this climax. The story of Jesus' death also completes and illustrates the meaning of everything else that has happened so far in the Gospel.

The Death of the Gospel Hero and Its Effects

There was darkness over the whole land until the ninth hour. And at the ninth hour Jesus cried with a loud voice, "Eloi, Eloi, lama sabachthani?" which means, "My God, my God, why have you forsaken me?" And some of the bystanders hearing it said, "Behold, he is calling Elijah." And one ran and, filling a sponge full of vinegar put it on a reed and gave it to him to drink, saying, "Wait, let us see whether Elijah will come to take him down" (15:33-36).

In true dramatic fashion, the total darkness from the sixth to the ninth hour forms the background and scene for Jesus' darkest hour. For special effect, Mark quotes Jesus' very last words in his own language, Aramaic: "Eloi, Eloi, lama sabachtani," which means, "My God, my God, why have you forsaken me?" These words may be a direct quotation of Psalm 22:1. Whether they are or not, they express the acute feeling of a final stage of abandonment: Judas, his friend and companion, has betrayed him; Peter, his chosen rock, has three times denied that he even knew him (14:66-71); all his male disciples have fled at his arrest (14:50). Now, to all appearances, God has forsaken him also.

Mark has directed all these descriptions to his persecuted audience. They too will feel abandoned by family and friends, as Jesus had predicted. Other Judases will deliver them over to Roman authority (13:12-13). They will see other Christians deny Jesus as Peter did, but they should not lose hope; even Peter, the worst betrayer, repented and was generously forgiven. Jesus' final words could very well express their own dereliction, for God seems to have abandoned them: "My God, my God, why have you forsaken me?"

Even these last words of Jesus are cruelly misunderstood by some bystanders, who think he is calling upon Elijah. The last words that Jesus hears from others seem also to be a jeering remark: "Wait, let us see whether Elijah will come to take him down" (15:36). These words are especially significant in view of the common Jewish belief that Elijah stood by the just in their dying moments in order to help them. Mark's audience would understand that, like Jesus, they should not expect any miraculous divine intervention in their last moments.

This temptation to expect quick, powerful delivery by God is the same temptation faced by Jesus, their teacher. In his dying moments he faced the triple diabolical temptation to come down from the cross in a great act of power to win a dramatic victory over his enemies and thus prove that he was the expected powerful Messiah of the Jews. First the passers-by shook their heads in derision and said, "Aha! You who would destroy the temple and build it in three days, save yourself, and come down from the cross!" (15:29-30). Then the chief priests and scribes mocked him, saying, "He saved others; he cannot save himself. Let the Christ, the King of Israel, come down now from the cross, that we may see and believe" (15:31-32). Finally, even Jesus' crucified companions taunted him in the same manner.

However, there is a surprising ending to Jesus' life that would give special hope to Mark's audience: ''But Jesus uttered a loud cry and expired. Then the temple veil was torn in two from top to bottom. When the centurion facing opposite him saw how he had thus (cried out and) died, he said, ''Truly this man was the [*or:* a] son of God'' (15:37-39).

Mark draws special attention to this last cry of Jesus before his death. It is mentioned twice (the second mention occurs in most Greek texts of 15:39). Whether or not the second is original, the large number of supporting Greek manuscripts suggests that from early times Jesus' death and last cry were the reason for the centurion's amazement and confession. Consequently, it is important to know how the centurion, along with the Gospel audience, would have understood the cry.

There is good evidence from Greek biblical usage that they would have understood Jesus' last cry as the final, triumphant shout of a hero.[10] This loud cry in Greek is *phonēn megalēn*. The New Testament in other places often has people, demons, or angels speak with such a ''loud voice'' to emphasize power and confidence, for example, Mark 1:26; 5:7; Luke 1:42; 17:15; 19:37; John 11:43, where Jesus calls Lazarus from the tomb with a loud voice; Acts 7:60, where the final loud voice and prayer of Stephen parallel those of Jesus. These texts show that Jesus' final, confident action was meant to be imitated by disciples undergoing the same ordeal. In the Book of Revelation we find that the expression ''a loud voice'' is used about sixteen times to emphasize power.

Following Jesus' last cry, the evangelist immediately proceeds to describe the effects of Jesus' death. This would be most important for the audience to know, since they face the same fate that Jesus did and would want to know what they could possibly accomplish by it. The first result of Jesus' death was the tearing, at least symbolic, of the Temple veil: ''Then the temple veil was torn in two from top to bottom'' (15:38).

This tearing of the veil could have several meanings, since there were two main veils: the outer veil of the Holy Place and

the inner veil separating it from the Holy of Holies.[11] Even for
a Greek or Roman audience, the torn veil would symbolize the
tearing down of exclusive Jewish access to God that was implied by the Temple. When the Romans celebrated their victory over the Jews in 71 A.D., their banners featured a representation of this torn veil.

Mark's audience would have been well aware that the outer
veil was not the most important one because each day the
priests went in and out of the Holy Place through this veil to
offer incense on the small altar in front of the inner veil, which
closed off the Holy of Holies. This inner veil was opened only
once a year in the most sacred action of the Jewish priesthood.
The high priest entered behind this veil with great fear to
sprinkle the blood of sacrifice on the holy ark for the atonement of sins, according to the ritual prescribed in the Book of
Leviticus (16:19-34). The Jews regarded this action as the great
exclusive privilege of their people.

The Holy of Holies was considered a symbol as well as a
pattern of God's dwelling in heaven. God instructed Moses
to build everything according to the pattern shown to him on
top of the mountain (Exod 26:30). Therefore, whatever was
done on earth before the ark of the covenant was believed to
be done in God's heavenly temple also. The tearing of the
Temple veil thus symbolizes complete and open access to God.
Previously, access to God had been the singular privilege of
the Jewish people, and thus the centurion could not obtain forgiveness and entry unless the barrier of the veil was broken
and access was extended to others.

To make this access possible, the death of Christ opens up
heaven by the symbolic tearing of the Temple veil. Then the
centurion can have a "conversion" through forgiveness and
can confess Jesus as the Son of God. In the Gospel of Mark,
he is the first person to do so. Actually, the whole Gospel has
been pointing toward the centurion's confession.[12] God's special action in the tearing of the veil is indicated by the Greek
passive voice (*eschisthē*) "it was torn" and the emphatic phrase

"from top to bottom." Mark uses the same verb to describe the opening of the heavens at Jesus' baptism, when the voice from heaven proclaimed him to be God's Son (1:11). Thus the beginning and the end of the Gospel are closely linked by these verbal parallels. In addition, the beginning and the end are connected to the middle of the Gospel, where a similar voice from heaven declares that Jesus is God's Son (9:7).

Another unusual detail about the centurion may have special significance. He is directly facing Jesus on the cross: he "stood facing him" (15:39). This expression is similar to that used for entering the Temple and standing in the presence of God. Mark may be telling us that the God whose presence was veiled in the Temple is now revealing himself through Jesus' death. Thus H. L. Chronis writes: "In his death, which culminates his mission of rejection and suffering (and thus satisfies the need of secrecy), Jesus manifests his true identity; and the effect, according to Mark, is equivalent to God himself showing his 'face.' "[13] This shows the connection between the destruction of the Temple and Jesus' revelation of himself: "According to Mark, it is Jesus—suffering, dying, rising—who is the true locus of the divine 'presence,' not the *sanctum sanctorum* of the Temple! Mark links Jesus' death (and the rejection and suffering leading to that death) with the end of the Temple because the revelation of God's 'face' *on the cross* shatters the Jewish cultus at its very foundation: worship 'before the face,' i.e., *in the temple.* "[14]

From the above descriptions, the audience would perceive the strong links between Jesus' death, the tearing of the veil, and the centurion's confession. Together they bring the Gospel drama to a climax. But would the audience have understood exactly *how* the death of Jesus accomplished this? Of course, if they immediately understood this death as a sacrifice, there would be no difficulty. We cannot just presume this, despite expressions about the Son of Man offering his life in ransom for many (10:45) and the pouring out of Jesus' blood at the Last Supper for many (14:24).

However, there are three important considerations that make us believe that Mark's audience saw Jesus' death as a sacrifice causing the centurion's confession. The first is based on the essential biblical ingredient of a sacrifice as a ritual action performed in obedience to God. For example, the most important sacrifice of all, that on the Day of Atonement, obtained its force from God's command to perform it in a detailed and prescribed way. The ritual concludes as follows: "And this shall be an everlasting statute for you, that atonement may be made for the people of Israel once in the year because of all their sins. And Moses did as the Lord had commanded him" (Lev 16:34).

There are similar words at the conclusion of the prescribed Passover rituals: "Thus did all the people of Israel; as the Lord commanded Moses and Aaron, so they did" (Exod 12:50). The essential matter of obedience appears in God's command to Abraham to sacrifice his only son Isaac. It was Abraham's willingness to obey God that was important, not the actual offering of his son, a sacrifice that God prevented him from making. Consequently, God swore to bless Abraham and to accomplish the divine promises through him for this reason: "because you have obeyed my voice" (Gen 22:18).

Because of the supreme importance of obedience in making any sacrifice effective, Mark makes it very clear to his audience that Jesus' death came about through such obedience to God and was voluntary as well. As examples, Jesus predicted his coming suffering and death three times (8:31; 9:31; 10:32-33). In the first prediction, the use of the Greek word *dei*, "it is necessary," implies that he was following a divine plan. Jesus also alludes to the scriptural plan of God when faced with the terrible shock that Judas, one of the Twelve, was about to betray him. Jesus said, "The Son of man goes as it is written of him, but woe to that man by whom the Son of man is betrayed" (14:21). In the story of Jesus' arrest, this obedience motif is especially stressed as Jesus prays to be able to do his Father's will and repeats again and again, "Not what

I will but what you will" (14:36, 39). Jesus explicitly states that his arrest was necessary in order that "the scriptures be fulfilled" (14:50).

A second reason prompting the audience to think in sacrificial terms is found in the parallels to Jesus' death in Jewish literature. In 2 Maccabees, the martyrdom of the mother of seven sons is explained as a means of bringing mercy and sacrifice to all the people. The last brother says before dying, "I, like my brothers, give up body and life for the laws of our fathers, appealing to God to show mercy soon to our nation and by afflictions and plagues to make you confess that he alone is God, and through me and my brothers to bring to an end the wrath of the Almighty which has justly fallen on our whole nation" (2 Macc 7:37-38).

The fourth book of Maccabees develops the same story by describing how the death of the brothers and their mother resulted in God's mercy and miracles; even the Greek tyrant is overcome by it and the whole land is purified.[15] The author writes, "Through the blood of those devoted ones and their death as an expiation, divine Providence preserved Israel that previously had not been afflicted." We cannot be sure that these texts had a literary influence on Mark or were known by the audience. However, they do portray ways of thinking about voluntary death as a sacrifice that would be current in Jewish Hellenistic circles.

The third consideration in understanding the causative effect of Jesus' death is that the language and expressions of Mark's Gospel would be familiar even to a non-Christian Greek and Roman world. Martin Hengel has assembled abundant literary evidence that Romans and Greeks alike thought of their heroes' deaths as bringing benefits, assistance, and even atonement to their friends as well as to the nation and others. Hengel makes the following conclusion: "The atoning death of the Son of God and reconciliation came about in the face of the imminent judgment of the world. All this was said in language and conceptuality which was not essentially strange to the men

of the Greek and Roman world. When fundamental difficul-
ties in understanding arise, they are felt not by the audience
of ancient times, Jewish or Gentile, but by us, the men of
today.''[16]

We can conclude, then, that Mark's audience would understand the death of Jesus as a sacrifice opening up the Holy
of Holies and making possible the conversion and confession
of the centurion. Likewise, they would understand that their
own persecution and martyrdom would likewise be an accept-
able prayer and sacrifice to God that could win over other ''cen-
turions'' and pave the way for Jesus' promised return. These
Christians would consider their own death as a sacrifice because it was in obedience to Jesus. The voice from the cloud
at Jesus' transfiguration had told them to listen to Jesus' words
on following him and taking up his cross. Therefore, the death
of the disciple is modeled on that of Jesus: Jesus made his witness and died in obedience to God and the Scriptures. The
ideal disciple could do the same by obeying the voice of God
directing him or her to follow Jesus' example.

The Dramatic Disclosure of the Counterparts of Jesus

So far we have presented Mark's view of the ideal disciple
in imitation of Jesus the Gospel hero. We have not mentioned
anyone who would be a counterpart of Jesus or emerge as a
model of the ideal disciple. We have proceeded in this way
to avoid confusion, since Mark's drama takes in a variety of
subplots. Now we wish to point out how Mark progressively
prepares the way for the disclosure of the secret counterpart
of Jesus.

Progressive Feminine Discipleship Models:
The First Two Dramatic Stages (Mark 1:1–3:6 and 3:7–12:44)

And immediately he left the synagogue, and entered the house
of Simon and Andrew, with James and John. Now Simon's
mother-in-law lay sick with a fever, and immediately they told

him of her. And he came and took her by the hand and lifted
her up, and the fever left her; and she served them (1:29-31).

The first cure by Jesus in Mark's Gospel is that of a notable
woman, the mother-in-law of Simon-Peter, his chief apostle.
She is also important because her house became the new home
and headquarters of Jesus at Capernaum. We call this a first
cure because Jesus' previous expulsion of an unclean spirit in
the synagogue (1:21-28) does not have the distinctive characteristics of Jesus' cures. Some of these are present in the cure
of Simon's mother: the hint of faith (in being told about Jesus);
the description of Jesus' taking her by the hand (1:31); the effect of the cure—the fever leaves her; and the immediate
resumption of her hospitality role. Although this cure begins
a sequence on feminine discipleship, it furnishes us few details about its special future meaning in Mark.

The Intermediate Phase of the Teacher/Disciple Sequence: The Teaching and Learning Chapters (Mark 3:7–12:44)

In this section Jesus' greatest and final healing is the raising of the daughter of Jairus, the account of which is inter-
twined with the story of the woman with an incurable
hemorrhage (5:35-43). The two stories go well together because
the second woman was "dead" also. She could never have
children because of this disruption of her fertility cycle. In addition, her illness made her perpetually unclean (Lev 15:25-27),
a social outcast who could never take part in worship or social
gatherings. She could only do so again after a "rebirth," when
the temple priests would certify that she was clean and would
offer sacrifice for her, as in the case of a leper (Lev 15:30).

In touching the two women, Jesus himself would incur the
worst ritual uncleanness. (In the case of Jairus' daughter,
touching a dead body would result in uncleanness for seven
days; see Num 19:12-16). Yet he does so and raises both
women to new life and the possibility of bearing children. The
young girl, the daughter of Jairus, was twelve years old, and

therefore legally able to marry. Both stories focus strongly on faith in Jesus despite impossible circumstances. The death-to-life theme is especially evident in both cases.[16] The number twelve in both stories (twelve years of hemorrhage and twelve years old) dramatizes their similarity.

The great tragedy of the loss of Jairus' daughter is evident in the father's attitude and the desperate mourning of the family and others. From Mark alone we could only guess that she might be an only daughter and thus the last hope to carry on the family name—a matter linked to life itself. Luke confirms what is implicit in Mark and calls her an only daughter (8:42). The mourning for such an only child would be especially acute. The story of the death of the only daughter of Jephthah and the yearly custom of bewailing her virginity may indicate a longstanding custom (Judg 11:34-40).

By way of anticipation, the two stories above prepare the way for the Gospel climax and Jesus' own death. At that time the great Gospel surprise will take place when an extraordinary faith will make possible an ideal disciple and counterpart of Jesus.

A fourth woman, a Gentile Syrophoenician, has a notable place in introducing the second multiplication of loaves with its symbolism of a bread destined for the non-Jewish world (7:24-30). The story hints at a special "insight" of the woman, since Jesus was hidden in a house and did not wish anyone to know about his presence (7:24). Yet somehow the woman has "inside knowledge"—she finds out where he is and comes to him for her daughter's cure despite the racial and religious barriers between Jew and Greek. She receives what seems to be a harsh refusal: "Let the children first be fed, for it is not right to take the children's bread and throw it to the dogs" (7:27).

Mark highlights the faith and humility of this woman, who trusted despite Jesus' apparent refusal. She replied, "Yes, Lord; yet even the dogs under the table eat the children's crumbs." She has the distinction of being singled out for direct praise from Jesus: "For this saying you may go your way; the demon has left your daughter" (7:29). In addition, her daughter's cure is the only one worked from a distance in Mark's Gospel. The woman returns home and finds her daughter lying in her bed cured. The deep faith of a Greek woman is thus presented as a model for the Gospel audience. It also prepares the way for Mark's fuller presentation of discipleship in the next and final division of the Gospel. These chapters, as the Gospel climax, will require more detailed study.

Extraordinary Discipleship Models in the Last Dramatic Sequence (Mark 13:1–16:8)

This section contains the final phase of the teacher/disciple relationship: Jesus' farewell and death. We suggest that the whole tone for Jesus' final testament in chapter 13 is set by a deliberate "inclusion," a literary device that links the beginning and end of a section by means of repetition. In dramatic presentation, this device focuses audience attention on their own response to Jesus' example. At the beginning we find the story of the poor widow, the fifth woman in our Markan series.

> And he sat down opposite the treasury, and watched the multitude putting money into the treasury. Many rich people put in large sums. And a poor widow came, and put in two copper coins, which make a penny. And he called his disciples to him, and said to them, "Truly I say to you, this poor widow has put in more than all those who are contributing to the treasury. For they all contributed out of their abundance; but she out of her poverty has put in everything she had, her whole living (12:41-44).

At the end of Jesus' last discourse, just before Judas' betrayal of Jesus, we have the story of the sixth woman in the series, the one at Bethany who anointed Jesus' head with oil as he sat at table (14:3-9). For study purposes, we will show the significant similarities of the two stories in parallel columns:

The Poor Widow	*The Bethany Woman*
1. The double mention of *poor* (12:42, 43).	1. The double mention of the poor (14:5, 7) in regard to selling ointment for the poor and "the poor you have always with you."
2. The double contrast to the rich and their offerings (12:41, 44).	2. The contrast to a rich offering of 300 denarii for the poor (14:5).
3. The widow gave all she had, *panta hosa eichen* (12:44).	3. The woman gave (all) she had, *ho eschen* (14:8).
4. The widow gave even "her whole life," *holon ton bion autēs* (12:44).	4. Jesus gives his life: "You will not always have me" (14:7).
5. Solemn amen conclusion (12:44).	5. Solemn amen conclusion (14:9).

The Bethany anointing is centrally located between Jesus' passion and his final testament in chapter 13. It has special meaning for the audience and sheds light on both Jesus' final testament and his death in view of Mark's dramatic crescendo. Elisabeth Schüssler Fiorenza describes the Bethany woman as Mark's portrait of the ideal disciple—one who understands who Jesus is and acts accordingly.[17] Peter had declared Jesus to be the Messiah but was rebuked for his failure to connect it with suffering and death (8:29-33). However, the Bethany woman anointed Jesus' head as a king but understood his messianic kingship in terms of his coming death.

In view of this portrait of discipleship, the following features of the story are significant, especially in light of the previous description of the widow. First of all, the whole atmosphere is enshrouded with the imminent prospect of Jesus' death. Just before the story the chief priests and scribes seek to arrest Jesus and kill him (14:14). Immediately after the account Judas meets with the chief priests to arrange for the betrayal of Jesus. In light of this context and the direct words of Jesus, the woman's anointment is a prophetic one in view of his death: "She has anointed my body *beforehand* for burying" (14:8). Jesus also mentions his death by saying, "You will not always have me" (14:7).

Another feature of the story is that the woman's action is participatory and teaches the nature of a true disciple. This emerges through the symbolism of the prophetic action. The ointment, *to myron*, is mentioned three times. It represents the woman herself as a "very costly" offering. This *myron* is at the same time connected to Jesus' death by a careful play on words: this *myron* (ointment) enables her to *myrisai* (anoint) his body for burial (14:8). Other allied symbolic elements reinforce this picture: the breaking of the vessel, a frequent symbol of death and destruction (e.g., Eccl 12:6; Jer 13:12-14); also, in Hellenistic times such "alabasters" containing ointment for burial were frequently left broken near the bodies of the deceased in burial places.[18] In addition, the action of pouring out symbolizes the giving of one's lifeblood (see Jesus' statement at the Last Supper that his blood will be "poured out"—14:24).

The Bethany story is so significant because it enters into the central Gospel question about Jesus' identity: *"Who do you say that I am?"* (8:29). Peter confessed Jesus to be the *Christos*, the Messiah or Anointed One, but he failed to accept the title as being connected with suffering and death; therefore he was rebuked by Jesus (8:28-33). This sequence is also linked to the meaning of discipleship, since Jesus immediately proceeds to talk about the necessity of taking up the cross and even losing one's life for his sake (8:34, 35).

In contrast to Peter's misunderstanding, the Bethany woman anoints Jesus' head and understands who he is. The anointing recalls the similar prophetic designation of kings or anointed ones in the Scriptures (1 Sam 10:1; 16:13). Yet she does this in view of Jesus' death, which Peter and the disciples found so difficult to accept (8:33-34; 9:33). In the Bethany account, some of them object to the woman's actions as follows: "Why was the ointment thus wasted?" (14:4). There seems to be much more than a question of wasting money, in view of Jesus' teaching on discipleship. In that context Jesus speaks of the loss or waste of one's own life (the same Greek root as in 14:4) in imitation of his own death (8:35). Thus the Bethany woman presents a full view of the ideal disciple: one who recognizes a suffering and dying Messiah, and one who gives her life in imitation. The latter idea is strengthened by the strong parallel to the poor widow's offering of "everything she had, her whole living" (12:44).

Once again with the widow's offering in mind, the Bethany woman's action represents an inner appreciation of discipleship, in contrast to the outer one of the disciples. In the widow's case, her one penny meant more than all the large offerings of the rich. For the Bethany woman, the same contrast appears: the ointment could have been sold for more than three hundred denarii to provide a rich offering for the poor (14:5). For Mark, the ideal disciple represented by the Bethany woman is one who recognizes *who Jesus is* and responds with a total personal offering of her/his life.

The final solemn amen statement by Jesus deserves special notice: "Wherever the gospel is preached in the whole world, what she has done will be told in memory of her" (14:9). This injunction of Jesus has not received proper attention. It has often been merely presented as a nice way of saying that the Bethany story should always be retold. Elisabeth Schüssler Fiorenza hit the mark when she said that the stories of Peter and the Twelve are well remembered; however, the story of the woman of Bethany is not, because it is not recognized as an essential part of the Gospel.[19] However, if Mark is presenting the woman of Bethany as ideal disciple, even in contrast to Peter and the others, her story is definitely an essential part of the Gospel.

Yet the total significance of the Bethany story and Jesus' statement about the worldwide preaching of the gospel can only be grasped through their connection with Jesus' final discourse in chapter 13. There, as we have already seen, Jesus foretells that the disciples' suffering and death will accomplish the necessary witness to the Gentiles that will precede and make possible Jesus' return.

In light of this central teaching of Jesus' last testament and discourse, the full meaning of the final amen statements of the poor widow's story and the Bethany account will emerge. The widow really gave everything she had, her whole life, as did the Bethany woman in appreciation of Jesus' death. This parallels the farewell statement of Jesus that "the one who endures to the end will be saved" (13:13). Such a witness, even unto death, will be the most effective *martyrion* to the rest of the world (13:9-10). Likewise, the story of the woman at Bethany will be told in the whole world because *the woman, as the ideal disciple imitating Jesus, makes such a preaching possible by her willingness to follow Jesus as far as the cross*. This confirms our previous statement that the story of the anointing at Bethany is indeed an essential part of the Gospel.

Finally, we should note the close similarity between the statements in 13:10 (the last discourse) and 14:9. The first one reads literally, "To all the nations (*ethnē*) first it is necessary that the gospel be preached." The words "it is necessary" (*dei* in the Greek) convey the meaning of a scriptural plan of God. In the conclusion to the Bethany story we have, "Wherever the gospel is preached in the whole world (*holon ton kosmon*), what she has done will be told in memory of her." There is a slight difference between the phrase "all the nations" in the first statement and "the whole world" in the second. This may be due to Mark's desire to closely parallel the two amen endings of the two women's stories. In the first the widow gave "all her life" (*holon ton bion autēs*), which corresponds to the second ending, "all the world" (*holon ton kosmon*). Thus Mark's brilliant rhetorical structure pushes the audience to conclude: *Only all of your life, like that of Jesus, will win all of the world*.

As part of Mark's dramatic crescendo, the woman at Bethany leads to the final counterpart of Jesus, since the ideal disciple must put into action what is prophetically presented by the anointing.

The Hidden Hero Identified in the Final Gospel Scenes (Mark 15:40–16:8)

First we should note that the whole Gospel of Mark depends on the eyewitness of Mary Magdalene and the other women. All the male disciples of Jesus had fled at his arrest (14:50). They were not ready to be arrested and crucified as followers of a suspected revolutionary. Judas had already betrayed his Master, and even Peter had denied him three times. Consequently, Mark carefully notes that the women were the sole witnesses not only of Jesus' death but of the place where he was buried and of the empty tomb.

To emphasize this witness, the author keeps repeating the verb "see." The women saw him actually die on the cross (15:40); they saw where he was laid (15:47); they saw the stone rolled back (16:4); they saw the young man dressed in white garments, who directed them to *see* the place where Jesus had lain (16:5,6). They were to tell the disciples that Jesus went before them into Galilee, where they would *see* him (16:7). All this takes place at great risk of being identified both at the cross and the burial place as friends and accomplices of a crucified revolutionary.

Mark is especially interested in describing Mary Magdalene and the other women in their climactic role of heroes and disciples: "There were also women looking on from afar, among whom were Mary Magdalene, and Mary the mother of James the younger and of Joses, and Salome, who, when he was in Galilee, followed him, and ministered to him; and also many other women who came up with him to Jerusalem" (15:40-41).

To make the portrait of the women as vivid as possible, Mark appears to be making parallels between the beginning and the end of the Gospel. Here there are several elements that have parallels in the original call of disciples in 1:16-20. First, there is the shadow of the cross, so evident in the above text and before the call of the disciples. There Mark notes that Jesus came into Galilee after John was arrested, a prelude to his death as a prophet, which Mark later describes in detail as a parallel to that of Jesus (6:14-29).

The second parallel is the emphasis on Galilee. The women had followed Jesus from Galilee (15:41). This corresponds to the double mention of Galilee in the first call. Jesus came into Galilee after John's arrest and found his first disciples by the Sea of Galilee.

As for the third parallel, Jesus called Peter, Andrew, James, and John, and "they followed him" (*ēkolouthēsan autō*—1:18, 20). The same Greek word is used of the women (*ēkolouthoun autō*—15:41). This following becomes especially significant by the added detail that they followed him to Jerusalem. This going up to Jerusalem is stressed several times: by the author (10:32); by Jesus in the third prediction of his death (10:33); and in the story of the blind Bartimaeus, who received his sight and followed Jesus on the way to Jerusalem (10:52–11:1). Another accessory link is the mention of Salome, whom the audience would recognize as the mother of James and John, who were among the first disciples called.

While making the link between the beginning and the end of his Gospel, Mark is also careful to keep the connections to the Bethany anointing. On that occasion Jesus stated that the woman "anointed my body beforehand for burying" (14:8). In the final story Mary Magdalene and the others came to "anoint him" (16:1). The story of the Bethany anointing and the portrait of ideal discipleship are completed in the story of Mary Magdalene and the other women. Mary Magdalene may possibly have been the same person as the woman at Bethany, but what is more important is that they certainly fulfilled the same role. Mary put into action what was symbolized by the woman at Bethany.

In addition, another very important parallel to the Bethany anointing appears in the amen ending that the story will be told "wherever the gospel is preached in the whole world" (14:9). We have already pointed out that the ideal disciple who suffers and even dies makes possible the necessary witness for the preaching of the gospel to the whole world, a prerequisite for the parousia. In the call of the first disciples this was stated in generic terms: "Follow me and I will make you become fishers of human beings" (1:17). However, now it is made specifically possible by the heroes who actually do follow Jesus as far as the cross. They are the ones whom the white-robed man at the tomb orders to tell the disciples that Jesus is going before them into Galilee, where they will see him (16:7).

This naming of Galilee is very significant, for it is the place where Jesus first gave his disciples the commission to be fishers of human beings. In view of the total mission orientation of Mark, Galilee is the gateway to the Gentile world.[20] Jesus' going before them into Galilee is meant to be an outreach to all the nations. It is the Gospel women who make possible this commission by following Jesus as far as the cross as images of the ideal disciple. Their inner realization of discipleship makes possible the outer work of preaching and teaching exemplified in the Twelve, though not exclusive to them by any means.

Of all the Gospel women, Mary Magdalene has a special claim to this title as the first named and leader of the women on all three occasions when they are mentioned (Mark 15:40, 47; 16:1). In support of this, John's Gospel later singles her out as the *only* woman as well as the only person to come to the empty tomb, see the risen Jesus, and take a special message to the disciples (John 20:1-18).

We cannot close without some discussion of our heroes in the final statement of Mark: "They went out and fled from the tomb; for trembling and astonishment had come upon them; and they said nothing to any one, for they were afraid" (16:8). This is the seemingly abrupt and enigmatic conclusion found in a number of important Greek manuscripts. The fact that the longer ending seems to be culled from verses in the other Gospels confirms the view that this verse was the original ending.

The sense of this closing statement, however, has remained

a puzzle for Scripture scholars and has resulted in tomes of research that we cannot possibly summarize here. The sense of the ending depends to a great extent on the view we have of the rest of Mark's Gospel. If our discipleship pattern rings true, it would at first seem unlikely that the Gospel would end with the women's failure to tell anyone about the extraordinary vision they saw and the words they heard at the empty tomb. That would seem to be direct disobedience to the directions of the young man clothed in white at the tomb (16:5).

Perhaps for the above reason, the earliest interpreters of Mark (the other three evangelists!) omit the difficult verse and give us a success story. In Matthew 28:8 the women run away to tell the disciples; in Luke 24:9-10 it is twice related that the women told the Eleven and the disciples; in John 20:14-18 we find that Mary Magdalene encounters the risen Christ, receives a special commission from him, and then goes to tell the other disciples.

If we have a ''success ending,'' the fear of the women is typical of the reaction to biblical epiphanies and should be expected. No disobedience or noncompliance should be implied. The final verse contains the customary Markan reaction against public disclosures; this does not exclude a particular communication to the disciples.[21]

There remains a lingering doubt about the women's behavior.[22] The final Gospel verse does seem to have a negative tone. However, the women's flight is explained in a sympathetic way by noting their great fear. Perhaps Mark wants to end with a divine success story, not a human one. Throughout the Bible, God works out divine plans despite weak human instruments. Perhaps there was also a flaw in our Gospel heroes, just as there was in Peter and the others. God's plans triumph despite the failure and contradiction of the cross, and despite the weaknesses of Jesus' disciples. This does not take away from our Gospel women; it rather enhances them as people with whom the audience, as ordinary people, can identify. Peter and the rest of the apostles had failed to understand the inner meaning of discipleship, in contrast to the women. Perhaps the women also did not measure up to the outer role of discipleship: announcing the word to others.

CHAPTER TWO

THE GOSPEL OF MATTHEW

"She has done a beautiful thing to me" (26:10)

Why Look at the Other Gospels?

Why should we look at the other Gospels at all if we have already found a hidden hero in Mark? The answer to this vital question must come from an understanding of the distinct nature of a Gospel. The Gospels are not mere variant reports about an earthly career; they are independent documents written a generation or more after Jesus' death. They were written to respond to the needs and problems of separate and distinct Christian communities. Consequently, each evangelist's presentation of the life and death of Jesus will be unique. The same will hold true of the hidden counterpart of Jesus in each Gospel.

As we did for Mark's Gospel, we will first study Matthew's audience. Then we will outline the portrait of the ideal disciple that emerges from that Gospel in light of the meaning of Jesus' death for the audience. Finally we will try to discover Matthew's hidden hero and her special characteristics.

The Situation and Problems of Matthew's Audience

Our method will involve contrast and comparison with Mark's Gospel. Mark addressed his Gospel primarily to a Greek, non-Jewish Christian audience. This was demonstrated by the author's explanation and translation of Jewish words, names, and customs. Also, for a Gentile audience Mark needed to appeal to a saying of Jesus to prove that Jewish laws of table fellowship no longer applied (7:19). In contrast, Matthew has no need to explain Jewish dress, customs, laws, and expressions. His Sermon on the Mount presumes that the audience is still observing the Jewish Torah. Jesus tells them that he has not come to destroy the Law but to bring it to perfection (5:17-20). For these and other reasons, it has been suggested that Matthew's audience was a largely Jewish-Christian community in dialogue and confrontation with official Judaism toward the end of the first century.[23]

In Mark's Gospel the atmosphere was that of a community under severe Roman persecution. The persecution in Matthew's Gospel originates mostly from fellow Jews rather than from Gentiles. This is shown by the principal persecution texts in chapter 10, which are Jesus' instructions for a mission to Jewish towns. In fact, Jesus distinctly forbids his disciples to enter Gentile territory (10:5). All this will affect Matthew's interpretation of Jesus' death for his audience. Their suffering and possible martyrdom will not be the principal means to win over the Gentiles, as they were for Mark.

Mark's audience had already broken away from Judaism to form a predominantly Gentile community. The Gospel's rejection texts point in this direction; for example, the vinedressers parable (12:8-10), the cleansing of the Temple to make place for all the nations (11:17), and the abrogation of Jewish food laws (7:19). However, despite similar rejection texts in Matthew's Gospel, his community seems to be very closely attached to Jewish ways, yet wavering regarding the question of authority.

This hesitation regarding the source of authority had its roots in the aftermath of the Jewish war with Rome (66–71 A.D.) and the resulting dilemma faced by Jewish Christians. The failure of Christians to fight against Rome (24:15-20) caused many Jews to brand them as traitors. This became a real obstacle toward winning further Jewish converts. In addition, after the war the Pharisees increasingly dominated Judaism, so their teaching and example became the norm for most Jews. This resulted in increasing friction with Jewish Christians, who no longer felt welcome in Jewish synagogues. The Jerusalem capital and Pharisaic leadership had been authoritative for Jewish Christians until the destruction of Jerusalem and the Temple in 70 A.D. Where could they go now for leadership, authority, and direction?

The crisis for Jewish Christians became even more acute as the number of Jewish converts dwindled. Jewish Christians often became a small minority within largely Gentile communities. Most of the latter did not share Jewish zeal and total dedication to the Torah and traditional Jewish practices. Many Jewish Christians were faced with the following choices: (1) to return to Judaism and their former Pharisee teachers; (2) to withdraw from Gentile Christians and establish independent, purely Jewish-Christian communities; (3) to follow Matthew's advice and accept new authoritative teachers along with God's plan for an increasingly Gentile apostolate.

Matthew's Portrait of the Ideal Disciple

What we previously wrote about Mark's Gospel as dramatic narrative applies equally to Matthew's. J. D. Kingsbury has brought this out very well.[24] As in Mark, the central character and hero of Matthew's Gospel is Jesus. All the events lead up to his death and its effects. In contrast, however, Jesus' last words and actions are not on the cross as in Mark. In Matthew, Jesus' death prepares the way for a final commission and his last words on a mountain in Galilee. This will be a key factor as we ascertain what effect the author intended Jesus' death to have on his audience. In turn, this will vitally affect Matthew's concept of the ideal disciple and, later on, his portrait of the Gospel's hidden hero.

Since the Gospel leads up to the death of its principal hero, Jesus, we will start with Matthew's version of the effects of his death:

And behold, the curtain of the temple was torn in two, from
top to bottom; and the earth shook, and the rocks were split;
the tombs also were opened, and many bodies of the saints who
had fallen asleep were raised, and coming out of the tombs after
his resurrection, they went into the holy city and appeared to
many. When the centurion and those who were with him, keeping watch over Jesus, saw the earthquake and what took place,
they were filled with awe, and said, "Truly this was the [or: a]
Son of God" (27:51-54).

For an audience trained in the Scriptures, the vivid images
of the splitting of the mountain, the opening of the tombs, and
the resurrection appearances were familiar. They were a dramatic representation that Ezekiel's well-known prophecy of the
dry bones coming to life had been fulfilled (Ezek 37:1-14). While
the prophecy originally meant that the "dead" Israel would
return from exile, it was commonly believed to be also a prophecy of the last times and of the resurrection of the dead. By
this description Matthew informs his audience that God has
intervened to vindicate Jesus' death and inaugurate the last
age of the world, in which the resurrection of the just would
take place. These events immediately precede the statement
of the centurion and others that Jesus is God's Son. Thus God
vindicates Jesus through these remarkable events in a way perceived by the centurion and those with him.

Matthew's special focus becomes clearer through a comparison with the centurion's confession in Mark's Gospel. In Mark
15:39 the centurion is deeply moved by *how* Jesus died: "When
the centurion . . . saw that he thus breathed his last [some
manuscripts add: and cried out], he said, 'Truly this man was
the (*or*: a) Son of God!' " Thus, as D. Senior has pointed out,
his statement is *revelatory*: the centurion is the first person in
Mark to really know who Jesus is by observing how he died.[25]
However, Matthew's view is quite distinct. In his Gospel, Jesus
is recognized as Son of God right from his birth and baptism:
the Magi come to worship the newborn child (2:11); Jesus' baptism is like a public proclamation: "This is my beloved Son"

(3:17). In contrast, Mark has a private revelation to Jesus in the words, "You are my beloved Son" (1:11). Thus, Matthew's purpose in the centurion's confession is not to announce a revelation but to proclaim a different *quality* of sonship.

This quality is first of all that of an obedient *Son* of God right up to the moment of death. Yet afterward this death is vindicated by mighty acts of God to show that Jesus then becomes Son of God in power and authority. The obedience motif starts with Jesus' temptation by Satan. In the desert the devil tempts him, "If you are the Son of God, command these stones to become loaves of bread" (4:3). Jesus replies, "A person shall not live by bread alone, but by every word that proceeds from the mouth of God." By these words Jesus contrasts a *powerful* Son of God and an obedient one who listens to the word of God. The second temptation begins in the same way, "If you are Son of God," followed by the suggestion to presume upon God's intervening with power. The third temptation ends with Jesus' response, "You shall worship the Lord your God and him only shall you serve" (4:10). These words imply absolute obedience to God in contrast to following the devil's plans for world domination through power.

The double temptation to use power has an intended dramatic counterpart at the cross. There the passers-by mock Jesus, "If you are the Son of God, come down from the cross" (27:40). The chief priests, scribes, and elders also join in, "He trusts in God; let God deliver him now, if he desires him; for he said, "I am the Son of God" (27:43). Even in his dying moments Jesus does not yield to this temptation. This goes along with Matthew's repeated stress that Jesus has fulfilled the Scriptures as a sign of obedience to God's plan. He is truly a Son of God according to the inner quality of a son. Of course, we must keep in mind that the word "son" or "child" had a much stronger connotation of obedience in the ancient world than it does today.

As with Mark, Matthew's story illustrates the results of Jesus' death in regard to the Gentile world as exemplified by the centurion. In fact, this is made even stronger by the addition of "those who were with him" (27:54). All of them are filled with fear at the great manifestation of power and make a *choral* confession that Jesus is the Son of God. This prepares the way for the Gospel ending, where Jesus directs the Eleven to make disciples of all the *ethnē* (nations), baptizing them in the name of the Father and the Son (28:19).

In addition, Matthew draws attention to a great change in the direction of salvation history. Jesus has been rejected as Son of God and mocked by official Jewish leaders right up to the end of his life. The portents that follow herald the inauguration of the long-awaited messianic age brought about by Jesus' resurrection. Hence the person of the risen Jesus becomes the center of faith. In contrast, in chapter 28 the Jewish elders and high priests reject the soldiers' testimony about the resurrection. Instead, they direct the guards to spread the story that Jesus' body was stolen while they were asleep (28:13). Then Matthew inserts a special message for his audience: "This story has been spread among the Jews to this day" (28:15). This statement implies a finality in official Jewish rejection of the resurrection. It also opens the way for Jesus' final statement about making disciples of all the nations, Jews as well as Gentiles (28:19). This new group will be gathered about the risen Jesus as authoritative Son of God in power.

We can now better understand the effect Matthew intended Jesus' death to have on his implied audience. First of all, they should personally realize how Jesus' obedience made possible his powerful title "*Son* of God." It was this obedience that prompted God to intervene with the earthquake and tomb openings, signifying the inauguration of the new age. This in turn resulted in the conversion of the Gentiles (the centurion and others).

Following Jesus' example, the audience's obedience and participation could have the same effect in promoting the preaching of the gospel to the Gentiles—a necessary prelude to the parousia (24:14). The *how* of this obedience will be taught in Jesus' last words on the Galilean mountain where he will transmit his teachings to his disciples so that they in turn can make disciples of all the nations (28:16-20). The guarantee of Jesus' presence, power, and authority would make this seemingly impossible task a reality.

For wavering Jewish Christians in the audience, other details of Jesus' death would also be very important. For this audience Matthew emphasizes the complete and absolute forgiveness afforded by Jesus' death. Jewish exclusiveness comes to an end with the symbolic tearing of the Temple veil. Forgiveness is now not only complete but is offered to all people, even the very Gentiles who had mocked and crucified Jesus. In addition, the audience would understand that the necessary means is the death *and* resurrection of Jesus. This last has been rejected by official Judaism, which spread false explanations of Jesus' empty tomb until the very day the audience listened to the Gospel (28:15). This means that wavering Jewish Christians can in no way go back to a Judaism that does not accept a risen Jesus.

By way of summary, we note the sharp distinction between Mark and Matthew. For Mark, to follow Jesus means to be willing to suffer and even die as a witness to convert the Gentiles. In Matthew, to follow Jesus means also to take part in his resurrection and accept his teachings as a new covenant to be brought to the whole world with all the authority and presence of Jesus the Son of God.

The Ideal Disciple in Matthew's Dramatic Narrative

Since the whole Gospel leads to Jesus' death and its meaning, the entire narrative must move toward this point. As in Mark, this will be accomplished in dramatic fashion according to the rules of rhetorical persuasion. These rely on a gradual crescendo, structural hints, and repetition until the whole Gospel is summed up in the closing scenes.

Drama depends on vivid images, so Matthew selects the most powerful images in his audience's memory to persuade them. His audience, in a pre-Gospel stage, had been taught through reading the Hebrew Scriptures. Perhaps the biblical event most strongly engraved upon their imagination was the flaming, trembling mountain of Sinai. Near Mount Sinai God had revealed his name to Moses from a burning bush. At this spot God had promised to lead the people out of Egypt so that they could come to this mountain to worship (Exod 3:1-12). God kept this promise. Then when the people arrived, they received the ten commandments as the mountain shook with God's thunderous voice accompanied by earthquake and fire (Exod 19:16–20:20).

As an artistic composer, Matthew chooses the powerful image of the mountain as an important vehicle to mark the dramatic progression of his Gospel.[26] Many key scenes in his narrative take place on a mountain: the devil takes Jesus to a high mountain to tempt him; in the Sermon on the Mount, Jesus, like a new Moses, gives his disciples his new Torah (chs. 5–7); on a mountaintop Jesus is transfigured before his disciples, and God's thunderous voice orders them to listen to (obey) Jesus (17:1-8); on the Mount of Olives, Jesus delivers his farewell address to his disciples (24:1); at the same location he makes the crucial decision to hand himself over to Judas for arrest (26:30). Finally, the last scene of the Gospel takes place on a mountaintop as Jesus commissions his disciples to go out to the whole world and promises that he will always be with them.

With the mountain image as a "stage setting," we will outline how the whole Gospel leads up to Jesus' death and the final mountain scene of commission. This will enable us to better appreciate Matthew's view of the ideal disciple, and in this context to discover the characteristics of the author's hidden hero. Matthew's first two chapters are essentially an infancy account to introduce Jesus as a new Moses.[27] There are corresponding tales of the unusual birth of each, the attempts to kill each child, and the journeys into Egypt. Even exact verbal correspondences occur, such as the command to return to Israel because those who sought the child's life are dead (2:20; cf. Exod 4:19).

The infancy stories really summarize the meaning of the Gospel and prepare for its ending. For example, Jesus' name at his circumcision means that he will save the people from their sins (1:21). This foreshadows the concluding death scene, where the torn veil of the Temple signifies forgiveness for all. The name Emmanuel, meaning "God is with us" (Matt 1:24), parallels the last words of the Gospel, "I am with you always" (28:20). With these words Jesus assures his disciples of the divine presence in their mission to bring his teachings to the world.

As in Mark's Gospel, God's voice pronounces Jesus to be God's Son at his baptism. However, in Matthew it resembles a public pronouncement for the audience: "This is my beloved Son" (3:17). Thus Jesus' role as obedient Son is clear from the beginning. As a cue, it prepares the audience for Jesus' death, when the centurion and others proclaim, "Truly this was the Son of God!" (27:54). However, the special meaning of "Son" emerges during Jesus' dramatic confrontation with Satan following his baptism. There Satan twice challenges Jesus with the words "If you are Son of God" (4:6, 7) and tempts him to be a Son of God characterized by power. The satanic temptation will return in Jesus' dying moments, when the bystanders as well as the chief priests taunt Jesus to come down from the cross if he is the Son of God (27:43). The temptation of Jesus is the first mountain scene in Matthew. Since the beginning of ancient drama often was connected to the end, the audience would look for a parallel to the concluding mountain scene in Matthew 28:16-20.

To discover this parallel, we must recall the Sinai mountain background Matthew has in mind for his audience. This is found first of all in God's call to Moses and the revelation of the divine name in Exodus 3:1-12. This key biblical text describes how Moses, exiled from Egypt to Sinai, was leading his flocks through the *desert* (as in Jesus' temptation) and drew near to "Horeb [Sinai], the mountain of God" (3:1). There Moses was amazed by the strange sight of a burning bush that was not being consumed by the fire. God then spoke to him from the fire. This was the God of Moses' fathers, who was about to save the suffering people in Egypt. To do this, God would send Moses to Pharaoh to obtain release for the people. Moses however responded, "Who am I that I should go to Pharaoh, and bring the children of Israel out of Egypt?" (3:11). God however answered, "I will be with you; and this shall be the sign for you, that I have sent you: when you have brought forth the people out of Egypt, you shall serve God upon this mountain" (3:12).

Already we can note the similarities to Jesus' temptation scene. In both cases the scene is the *desert* (Exod 3:1; Matt 4:1). Next, Jesus' last temptation takes place on a *mountain*. At Mount Sinai we also have a temptation motif as Moses hesitates and questions God. In both stories the essential matter is worship on the mountain. Jesus answers the devil, "You shall worship the Lord your God and him only shall you serve" (4:10). Likewise with Moses, God promised him a special sign that he and the people would return to worship at Sinai: "I will be with you; and this shall be the sign for you, that I have sent you: when you have brought forth the people out of Egypt, you shall serve God upon this mountain" (Exod 3:12).

God fulfilled this promise by going before the people in a pillar of fire, leading them out of Egypt and back to Mount Sinai (Exod 13:21). When they arrived there, God made a special covenant with them and gave them the ten commandments. Then God called Moses, Aaron, and the other leaders to ascend Mount Sinai while the people worshiped from afar (Exod 24:1). The Greek Bible text uses the same word for "worship" here as is found in Jesus' temptation (4:10) and in the concluding worship of Jesus on the mountain in Galilee (28:17).

From the above scriptural background we can better understand the striking correspondence between the beginning and the end of Matthew's Gospel. On the mountain of temptation

Jesus declares that he will serve and worship God alone (4:10);
at the end of the Gospel the disciples worship Jesus (28:17).
Jesus commissions them to teach what he has commanded
them (similar to Moses and the people) and assures them with
a final word, "I will be with you" (28:20), the same words that
God said to Moses (Exod 3:12). At Jesus' temptation he was
promised authority over all the earth if he followed the devil's
plans (4:9); on the mountain in Galilee Jesus tells his disciples,
"All authority in heaven and on earth has been given to me"
(28:18). This is because he has followed God's plans, even
when they led to the cross and death, not the devil's plans
for him to use power. Finally Jesus can send his disciples out
to win over the whole world.

These remarkable parallels between the beginning and the
end show that the whole Gospel leads to a dramatic climax
at the final mountain scene. Yet it is Jesus' death and the con-
sequent events that make it possible. We can now outline how
the rest of the Gospel prepares the way for this and get a better picture of Matthew's ideal disciple.

The journey of the audience to the final mountain begins
with Jesus' call of the disciples/audience by the Lake of Galilee.
Jesus commanded them, "Follow me, and I will make you fishers of human beings" (4:19). Disciples must follow the same
path that Jesus took. Just as he pledged complete obedience
to God on the mountain of temptation, so the disciples must
obey Jesus and follow him even to the cross. Since we have
already noted this emphasis in Mark, it will not be necessary
to point out the parallel passages in Matthew's Gospel.

Like Moses, who led the people up Mount Sinai to receive
God's commandments, so also Jesus leads his disciples up a
mountain in 5:1. There the Sermon on the Mount contains
Jesus'own words and commands in antithesis to God's words
to Moses on Mount Sinai. For example, "You have heard that
it was said to the people of old, 'You shall not kill; and whoever kills shall be liable to judgment.' But I say to you that every
one who is angry with his brother shall be liable to judgment"

(5:21-22; see also 5:27, 31, 33, 38, 43). Thus Jesus takes on the role of a new Moses with new commandments going far beyond what the Pharisees taught. Through this, Jewish Christians in the audience would find guidance for a new way surpassing that of their former teachers. The mountain sermon ends with a literary seam: "When Jesus finished these sayings, the crowds were astonished at his teaching, for he taught them as one who had authority, and not as their scribes" (7:29). These words stress the authority of Jesus' words in contrast to those of Jewish teachers. The descent from the mountain in 8:1 sets off the Sermon on the Mount as a distinct literary unit and a summary of Jesus' teachings.

Chapters 8 and 9 are a collection of ten miracles of Jesus. They confirm Jesus' authority. Matthew's miracles have only a fraction of the details found in Mark's Gospel. The evangelist seems to have deliberately trimmed them to focus on Jesus' *word* and his *person*. Matthew's stories are encounters with Jesus' person that bring out the power of his words. For example, the cure of the centurion's servant (8:5-13) has similarities to the outcome of the Gospel. The centurion is so impressed by the authority and power of Jesus' word that he says to him, "Only say the word, and my servant will be healed" (8:8). Jesus cures even from a distance, just as his words at the end of the Gospel reach out and "cure" the distant world.

The concluding words of the story of the centurion really sum up the Gospel's effect: "Many will come from east and west and sit at table with Abraham, Isaac, and Jacob in the kingdom of heaven, while the children of the kingdom will be thrown into the outer darkness" (8:11-12). These words foreshadow the final mountain scene. Under Jesus' command the disciples/audience are to invite everyone to a final messianic banquet, at which both Jews and Gentiles will be present. The exclusive place of Israel is at an end.

Matthew's second great discourse, often called Jesus' missionary instructions, is found in chapter 10. Here Matthew does relate that Jesus called his twelve Jewish disciples, gave them special powers, and sent them on a mission that did *not* at first include Gentiles and Samaritans: "Go nowhere among the Gentiles, and enter no town of the Samaritans, but go rather to the lost sheep of the house of Israel" (10:5-6).

However, the mission appears to be temporary and unsuccessful, for Jesus predicts that the disciples will not finish going through the towns of Israel before the Son of Man comes (10:23). Also, the apostles are not allowed to *make disciples*, as Jesus does; the command to make disciples will come only at the final mountain scene, after Jesus' death has made possible a joint community of Jews and Gentiles. In contrast to Mark's Gospel, the persecutions on this mission will come mostly from fellow Jews, and only incidentally from Gentile rulers (10:17-18). So Mark's concentration on suffering and martyrdom as promoting the conversion of Gentiles is not prominent in Matthew's Gospel. This will mean a marked difference in Matthew's view of discipleship. Words and actions will receive much more emphasis in his Gospel.

In chapters 11 and 12 the audience will receive more hints and preparation for the coming death of Jesus and its effects. These chapters concentrate on Jesus' preaching, his rejection, and the transmission of the gospel to others. For example, Jesus' healing on the Sabbath ends with the Pharisees' counsel to destroy him (12:14). Matthew appears to be emphasizing the opposition of the Pharisees to warn his audience. They need to know that their former teachers were hardly in sympathy with Jesus and his teaching. Such hints of Jesus' death prompt his withdrawal and a quotation from Isaiah about a suffering servant of the Lord who "shall proclaim justice to the Gentiles" (12:18). Finally, Jesus' clear announcement of the sign of Jonah to the Pharisees (12:38-41) makes the hints more explicit. God had forced Jonah, the comic Hebrew prophet, to preach to the Gentiles. Jonah found it extremely hard to accept a God who could be loving and merciful even to the enemies of the Jews.

Matthew's next great discourse is his special collection of parables (13:1-51). These also prepare the audience for Jesus' death and its effects; open forgiveness for all is an important element in that scene. In the parable of the weeds and the wheat (13:24-30, 36-43), God desires the evil weeds (sinners) to grow together with the wheat until the time of the harvest and judgment. In the parable of the fishnet (13:47-50), the net collects all kinds of fish, good and bad; the process of selection and judgment comes later. For Matthew, this theme of general invitation and forgiveness is distinctive of Jesus and contrary to Pharisee exclusivism.

As in Mark, the Baptist's martyrdom foreshadows Jesus' own. It emphasizes the need for succession, which will be brought out through the double cycle of miracles of feeding, first five thousand and then four thousand people. The disciples will have a key role in making Jesus' presence continue through a new bread that will unite both Jews and Gentiles. While Mark stresses the bread itself, Matthew centers the miracles of feeding more on Jesus as teacher and giver of bread, because he wants to show a contrast between Jesus' universal bread and the separatism of Pharisee teachers.[28] To confirm this, the two miracles of the loaves in Matthew conclude with the story of the disciples who had forgotten to bring bread with them in the boat. Jesus warns them against the "leaven of the Pharisees and Sadducees," which Matthew interprets in reference to their teachings (16:11-12).

Once again, in the miracles of feeding the authority and power of Jesus' person come out in a way especially related to Jesus' death and the subsequent powerful confession, "Truly you are the Son of God." Only after Jesus' death and after the miracles of loaves is this title given to Jesus by human beings. Matthew prepares for this by another favorite mountain scene showing Jesus at prayer after the first miracle of loaves. From the mountain Jesus sees his disciples in trouble in a boat at sea because of a strong wind. He comes down to help them by walking on the water—a hint of his death and resurrection. Peter starts to follow him across the water but loses courage, begins to sink, and cries out, "Lord, save me." Jesus then takes him by the hand and rescues him, bringing him into the boat. At that point "those in the boat worshiped [Jesus], saying, 'Truly you are the Son of God' " (14:33).

This first confession of Jesus as the Son of God centers on his power and authority over the sea and the powers of death. It prepares the way for the following authoritative teaching of Jesus about breaking the barriers preventing Jewish and Gentile table fellowship. Peter's important part in this matter seems to be brought out by his question about it (15:15).

The second confession (16:16) follows the second feeding and builds further on the contrast between Jesus' teaching and that of the Pharisees and Sadducees. It is also initiated by Peter. This second confession envisions an authority that conquers even death: "the powers of death shall not prevail against it" (16:18). It also centers on Peter's teaching authority and that of his successors (since Peter himself was no longer alive when Matthew wrote): "I will give you the keys of the kingdom of heaven, and whatever you bind on earth shall be bound in heaven, and whatever you loose on earth shall be loosed in heaven" (16:19).

The above confessions of faith anticipate the centurion's final confession after Jesus' death. They emphasize the power and authority of Jesus as Son of God, especially in his victory over death and in his teaching office. This will be very important for Jewish Christians in the audience who need a new, secure authority after the split from Judaism and the destruction of the Temple.

Like Mark, Matthew gives central importance to Jesus' three predictions of his suffering, death, and resurrection. Each is followed by a collection of Jesus' teachings on discipleship. Likewise, these difficult words of Jesus are emphasized for the disciple/audience by another mountain scene, that of the transfiguration. There a heavenly voice enjoins the disciples to obey Jesus' words: "This is my beloved Son, with whom I am well pleased; listen to him'' (17:5). However, Matthew makes some important modifications that will shape his distinct view of the ideal disciple.

These changes are as follows. In Mark we noted that the sequence of Jesus' suffering, death, and resurrection was paralleled by the persecution, death, and participation in the parousia by the disciple. This is brought out by the words, ''Whoever is ashamed of me and of my words . . . of that person will the Son of man also be ashamed, when he comes in the glory of his Father with the holy angels'' (8:38). In contrast, Matthew only appeals to a final judgment: ''The Son of Man is to come . . . and then he will repay every one for what he or she has done'' (16:27). This hints that Matthew's emphasis is more on what people actually do than on the personal witness of martyrdom.

The greatest difference in Matthew's triple cycle of discipleship is the addition of an entire discourse, chapter 18, on church discipline and authority in regard to sin and forgiveness, a matter especially connected with Jesus' death. Breaking from the Pharisees' practice, Jesus' disciples must search out the lost sinners like a shepherd who leaves ninety-nine sheep in the mountains to look for even one that is lost. The basic attitude should be joyful finding and reconciliation (18:14).

Applying the same attitude, the continually lapsing sinner who wears out everyone's patience is to be forgiven not seven times but seventy times seven times (18:21). Even the hardened sinner must be provided every possible opportunity, first by private exhortation, then by two or three witnesses, and finally by the whole church (18:15-20). The church's authority in regard to sin and forgiveness is God's own authority: ''Whatever you bind on earth shall be bound in heaven, and whatever you loose on earth shall be loosed in heaven'' (18:18). The source of this authority is Jesus' presence in community gatherings: ''Where two or three are gathered in my name, there am I in the midst of them'' (18:20). This presence of Jesus'

person, an important and distinctive Gospel theme, is emphasized at the beginning (with the name Emmanuel, "God with
you," in 1:23) and at the end with Jesus' promise, "I am with
you always" (28:20).

After the discipleship sequence Matthew has Jesus' entry
into Jerusalem, the cleansing of the Temple, and Jesus' conflict situations and dialogue with Jewish authorities. Compared
with Mark, Matthew has sharpened these, focusing on the
Pharisees' role. This whole section, as well as the Gospel
proper, concludes with a long, scathing condemnation of the
Pharisees in chapter 23. There the Pharisees' example is con-
demned as a model for others to follow; their opposition to
Jesus fits into a long tradition of opposition to prophetic teachings. This culminates both in the loss of God's Temple and
in the loss of Jesus' own presence among them (23:34-39). This
last statement serves as an introduction to Jesus' last discourse
and final testament to his disciples in chapters 24-26. There
Jesus will instruct the disciples as to how his presence will continue among them.

This final farewell address of Jesus takes place on another
mountain, the Mount of Olives, in chapters 24-25. The differences from Mark's version are very significant for Matthew's
view of discipleship. In Mark 13:9-10 the author described the
persecution and death of the disciple as a *martyrion* to the Gentiles so that the gospel might be preached to all the nations.
The disciple is encouraged to persevere until the end (of life)
in 13:13. However, in Matthew this clear link between the disciple's *martyrion* and the preaching of the gospel is missing.
Instead, the words of Jesus in the Gospel are the witness: *"This
gospel* of the kingdom will be preached throughout the whole
world, as a testimony to all nations; and then the end will
come" (24:14).

This new stress on keeping the words of the gospel rather
than on giving one's life for it can be better understood in view
of the different time perspectives in Matthew and Mark. In
Mark, time is short and the audience anxiously awaits Jesus'

return. Therefore the best witness is to give one's life during Gentile persecution. In Matthew, however, Jesus' return has been delayed and the audience is not primarily faced by Gentile persecution; hence the essential matter will be keeping the authoritative and powerful words of Jesus, which last forever.

The following texts support this delay of Jesus' return in Matthew's Gospel. In a parable the servant in charge of the household begins to mistreat his fellow servants and consorts with drinkers because he thinks, "My master is delayed" (24:48). The ten maidens fall asleep because "the bridegroom was delayed" (25:5). In the parable of the talents, the master returns to settle accounts "after a long time" (25:19). In each case Jesus advises vigilance in prayer and concentration on good works. The Master certainly will return, but the time is unknown and most people will be caught unprepared (24:42-44, 50; 25:13).

This urgency of good works and vigilance reaches a peak in the concluding scene of the judgment of nations, which is found only in Matthew (25:31-46). The passage is very important because it contains Jesus' final words in the Gospel before the passion account begins. Matthew's judgment scene has many surprises: Israel is not judging the nations, as is the common view; instead, the nations are witnesses.

This view appears in Jesus' Sermon on the Mount, where disciples are challenged to be the salt of the whole earth and the light of the world; their good works should be so evident that observers would glorify God because of them (5:14-16). In Matthew 25 the judge of the world does not ask if people are circumcised or if they have kept the biblical laws. Nor is there any mention of special benefits for Christian charismatics who "prophesy . . . and cast out demons . . . and do many mighty works" (7:22) in Jesus' name. Instead, we have simple examples of obedience[29] to Jesus' word, such as feeding the hungry in accord with his command, "You give them something to eat," at the multiplication of loaves (14:16), or giving drink to the thirsty (10:42). In other words, obedience to Jesus' command to feed the hungry is a direct service to him. This is an important and distinctive element in the judgment for Matthew's Christian audience. It will also be closely linked with the next episode on the anointing at Bethany, which will be studied in connection with the Gospel hero.

This distinctive new element for the audience/disciple needs further explanation. There is nothing new about feeding the hungry, giving drink to the thirsty, welcoming the stranger, and clothing the naked. Matthew and the audience would certainly know Isaiah 58:6-9, where the prophet describes what must accompany fasting for God if a response to prayer is to be expected: "Is it not to share your bread with the hungry, and bring the homeless poor into your house; when you see the naked, to cover them, and not to hide yourself from your own flesh?"

In Isaiah these works of mercy are regarded as direct service to God. We find the same view elsewhere, especially in Deuteronomy. For example, loving and serving God are equated with obedience and keeping God's commandments (10:12-13; 11:13; 13:5; 24:24). This is especially true regarding justice for the orphan and the widow or feeding and clothing the alien—all these are regarded as a direct personal service to God: "[The Lord your God] executes justice for the orphan and the widow, and loves the sojourner, giving him or her food and clothing. Love the sojourner therefore; for you were sojourners in the land of Egypt. You shall fear the Lord your God; you shall serve the Lord your God" (Deut 10:17-20).

Going now to Jesus' commands, we have already seen in the Sermon on the Mount that Matthew places them side by side with God's commandments. Just as obedience to God was a direct personal service to God in the Old Testament, so obedience to Jesus' commands becomes a direct personal service to him and to God. For this reason the judgment narrative keeps repeating the words "me" or "to me" on the part of Jesus—some twenty times in all. It starts off with, "I was hungry and you gave *me* food, I was thirsty and you gave *me* drink, I was a stranger and you welcomed *me* . . ." (25:35f.).

For unforgettable emphasis, the whole series is repeated in question form by the just: "When did we see you hungry and feed you . . . ." Then it is all summarized by Jesus' statement, "As you did it to one of the least of these . . . , you did it to me" (25:40). Finally the whole dialogue occurs again in a negative form with Jesus' conclusion, "Amen, I say to you, as you did it not to one of the least of these, you did it not to me" (25:45). The element of personal service is strengthened by the use of the verb *diakonein*, "to minister or serve." This occurs in the second group, when those on the left side ask, "Lord, when did we see you hungry or thirsty or a stranger or naked or sick or in prison, and did not *minister* to you?" (25:44).

Jesus' last discourse, in chapters 24 and 25, moves into the passion account with the literary joiner, "When Jesus had finished *all these sayings* . . ." (26:1). The four previous discourses have similar endings (7:28; 11:1; 13:53; 19:1). However, the word "all" was not used previously. Probably Matthew meant to include all the previous discourses by using this word. If so, Matthew's five discourses are a compendium of Jesus' teachings, which are to be taught to all the world (28:20) after his death.

The passion account opens with a contrast between the plot to betray Jesus (26:3-5) and a woman's extravagant anointing of him at Bethany (26:6-13). Matthew's special treatment of this will be found later in our special study of the Gospel hero. The author's Last Supper account once more focuses on the person of Jesus. Jesus knows who the betrayer is, and even identifies him (26:25). Despite this, Jesus goes ahead and offers himself in the symbolic form of bread and wine. In this way Matthew may be hinting that Jesus offers himself even for his betrayer and worst enemy. Thus Jesus practices his own teaching, "Love your enemies," found in the Sermon on the Mount (5:44). Further emphasis is placed on the person of Jesus and his words by an added verbal quotation of Jesus' commands to both eat the bread and drink the cup. Also, Jesus' specific words are added: "for the forgiveness of sins" in connection with the cup (26:28). This reminds the audience that it is the person of Jesus, especially his saving blood, that brings forgiveness of sins.

The scene then moves to another favorite mountain, the Mount of Olives, where Jesus' final decision about his arrest and death will be made. At this point Matthew starts preparing for the final mountain theophany by giving the first of three predictions or commands. Jesus predicts that all the disciples will fall away and then says, "It is written, 'I will strike the shepherd, and the sheep of the flock will be scattered.' But after I am raised up, I will go before you to Galilee" (26:31-32). This "going before to Galilee" will also be announced by the angel at the empty tomb (28:7), and a third time by the risen Jesus to the women (28:10). Finally, the author will note its accomplishment: "Now the eleven disciples went to Galilee, to the mountain to which Jesus had directed them" (28:16). There is no doubt that Jesus' death makes possible the final Gospel sign—the worship and commission on the mountain in Galilee. This forms a remarkable parallel to God's sign to Moses that the people would return to the mountain (of Sinai) to worship (Exod 3:12).

In view of our purpose, it will not be necessary for us to discuss the arrest of Jesus and his trials before Pilate and the high priest. These set in motion the final decisions that lead to Jesus' death, which we have already discussed. Instead, let us move to the culminating mountain scene at the end of the Gospel, toward which the whole drama has been moving.

The Final Mountain Christophany

Matthew's final mountain scene in 28:16-20 is the culminating point of the Gospel. The author skillfully presents this as a final sign to the audience/disciples that Jesus has fulfilled the triple promise to lead them there (26:32; 28:7, 10). This is a dramatic parallel to God's promised sign to Moses that the people would worship on Mount Sinai (Exod 3:12).

"Now the eleven disciples went to Galilee, to the mountain to which Jesus had directed them. And when they saw him they worshiped him, but some doubted" (28:16). The audience, especially Christian teachers, could certainly identify with the eleven disciples. Even though the latter were no longer alive, their teaching office continued in others. This is because Jesus, the authoritative teacher, remains with his disciples even to the close of the age, which, we noted, is delayed in the Gospel of Matthew. The Eleven worship Jesus on the mountain, just as Moses and the elders returned to worship God on Mount Sinai (Exod 24:1-2) in fulfillment of God's promise and command.

"And Jesus came and said to them, 'All authority in heaven and on earth has been given to me'" (28:18). Jesus now appears on a new Mount Sinai to take God's place as authoritative Son of God (Father and Son are named in the next verse). At first glance, the ancient "fireworks" theophany of Mount Sinai seems to be missing: "The Lord descended upon it [Mount Sinai] in fire: and the smoke of it went up like the smoke of a kiln, and the whole mountain quaked greatly" (Exod 19:18). Matthew has the same theophany images but spreads them out: the earth shakes at Jesus' death and also at the opening of his tomb (27:51; 28:2); the Greek word for "lightning" (*astrapai*) in Exodus 19:16 is the same word that describes the angel at Jesus' tomb: "His appearance was like lightning, and his raiment white as snow" (28:3). Thus the fire-and-lightning theophany at Sinai takes place at the empty tomb.

These links to Sinai would certainly be recognized by Matthew's audience. Matthew probably also had in mind the triple mention of the "third day" in the Sinai theophany (Exod 19:11, 15, 16), which paralleled Jesus' own resurrection on the third day. These signs encourage the disciples/audience to have ab-

solute confidence in Jesus' power and authority as Son of God
to accomplish the new mission he is entrusting to them.

"Go therefore and make disciples of all nations, baptizing
them in the name of the Father and of the Son and of the Holy
Spirit" (28:19). The authoritative command "Go" issued by
the Son of God provides the disciples/audience with the commission and the power for the new task ahead. The injunction "make disciples" (mathēteusate) is now given to the
disciples for the first time. It is new because it is now to include "all nations" (panta ta ethnē). This makes it clear that
Jesus' ultimate goal is a joint community of Jews and Greeks.
The cross and resurrection have broken down all exclusivism.
The word "baptizing" puts Jew and Gentile on an equal plane.
Both need forgiveness of sins, which is linked to this baptism.

". . . teaching them to observe all that I have commanded
you" (28:20). Jesus' teaching authority as Son of God has already been announced by his words to Peter at Caesarea Philippi (16:16-19). On Mount Sinai, God gave his covenant and
commandments to Moses; here Jesus entrusts his disciples with
his *new covenant* of instructions. Matthew has already summarized these in his five great discourses. On Mount Sinai, Moses
took the book of the covenant and read it to the people. They
in turn responded: "All that the Lord has spoken we will do,
and we will be obedient." Moses then took blood, sprinkled
it upon the people, and said, "Behold the blood of the covenant which the Lord has made with you in accordance with
all these words" (Exod 24:7-8). In like manner, the *observance*
of Jesus' commandments has been a continual theme throughout the Gospel of Matthew.

"I am with you always, to the close of the age" (28:20).
These are Jesus' final words in the Gospel. They are a remarkable parallel to God's guarantee to Moses to bring the people
back to Mount Sinai for worship: "I will be with you; and this
shall be the sign for you: when you have brought forth the
people out of Egypt, you shall serve God upon this mountain"
(Exod 3:12). They are now God's words in Jesus forming an

inclusio (literary bracket) with the beginning of the Gospel. There it was noted that God's plan was to call the awaited Messiah "'Emmanuel,' which means, God with us" (1:23).

Because of this promise of Jesus' continual presence, the implied audience/ideal disciple would *hear* Jesus' words throughout the Gospel as actually addressed to them. In this way hearing Matthew's Gospel would be an *experience* of Jesus' presence. Likewise, when they heard the powerful word of the Son of God, they would feel themselves empowered both to keep these commands and to courageously undertake Jesus' commission for a worldwide apostolate to break down ethnic barriers between Jew and Greek. No doubt the audience would listen to the Gospel again and again. Each time they did, they would receive new insights as well as experience anew Jesus' presence. This *energy* was a primary concern in the Hellenistic world, where grace and Jesus' words would be perceived in terms of energy flow.[30]

We can now sum up the differences between Mark and Matthew in reference to the meaning of Jesus' death and discipleship. Mark was greatly influenced by the crisis caused by Roman persecution. Believers awaited Jesus' return within a short time to vindicate them. Mark presented Jesus' obedient and voluntary death as the supreme example for disciples. It was the death of a victorious martyr who even elicited a confession of faith from a Gentile centurion. In the same manner, the greatest privilege of the disciple/audience is to suffer and even die as Jesus did, in obedience to him. This will be the best way to win over other Gentiles and to fulfill the necessary condition for the return of Jesus. In the meantime, the community endures the temporary absence of Jesus, except in the new meaning of ritual breaking of bread in anticipation of his speedy return.

Matthew's community faces a different crisis. The parousia has been indefinitely delayed. The audience undergoes persecution predominantly from fellow Jews, not Gentiles. This means that the best way to win over the world will not be through heroic martyrdom but by good deeds and actions. Jewish Christians are also faced with the tendency to exclusivism. In response to this, Matthew focuses on the power and authority of Jesus' person. In his description of Jesus' death, he brings out a dual meaning of the title "Son of God." Jesus is Son of God through his obedience to his Father even unto death, yet he becomes Son of God in power through his resurrection. This means that he is also an authoritative teacher, much greater than Moses. As such, he provides the community with instruction and guidance through his successors, the Twelve, and the teachers who come after them.

Jesus' death seals a new covenant composed of his words and commands. These provide a new way not only for Jewish Christians but for the whole world, which is offered complete forgiveness through the cross. As in Mark, the risen Jesus is indeed present in community gatherings, but with special emphasis on the bestowal of forgiveness. Matthew, however, brings out that at other times Jesus is not absent but is present to believers each time they listen to Jesus' teachings and commands with a sincere desire to put them into practice. This practice has a new, distinctive element for Christians. Care for the poor, the hungry, the homeless, the sick, and those in need becomes a personal service to Jesus himself and is the best way to remember him in daily life.

The Secret Hero of Matthew's Gospel

Once again, as we did with Mark's Gospel, we will look for a pattern in the progressive stories of women in Matthew's Gospel that will lead us to his hero and understand her better. We have just finished studying Matthew's audience and his portrait of the ideal disciple. This will be very important in discovering the unique traits that his Gospel hero will have. They will be in conformity with Matthew's special message for his audience.

In tracing this pattern, we will start with the cure of Peter's mother-in-law. We will not begin with Mary, the mother of

Jesus, because Matthew gives us little about her that would help us to see or understand her as a person or disciple. We must wait for the Gospel of Luke to do this. For Matthew, Mary is extremely important as the mother of the Messiah and as the fulfillment of God's plan in history. However, in the stories about her, Matthew focuses on Joseph and the mother/child as the completion of God's scriptural plan.

For study purposes, we will better appreciate Matthew's view of the role of women in his Gospel through comparison with Mark's and by sometimes placing the texts of Matthew and Mark in parallel columns.

The Healing of Peter's Mother-in-Law

Matthew 8:14-15	*Mark 1:29-31*
And when Jesus entered Peter's house, he saw his mother-in-law lying sick with a fever; he touched her hand, and the fever left her, and she rose and served him.	And immediately he left the synagogue, and entered the house of Simon and Andrew, with James and John. Now Simon's mother-in-law lay sick with a fever, and immediately they told him of her. And he came and took her by the hand and lifted her up, and the fever left her; and she served them.

The distinct differences between Matthew and Mark in this brief story reveal Matthew's special interests. We notice that he highlights the power and person of Jesus, a typical practice in his Gospel. First, he substitutes the name Jesus for the personal pronoun "he." He does this some eighty times in passages parallel to Mark's Gospel. Second, we read in Matthew that Jesus touched the hand of Peter's mother-in-law and the fever left her. The mere touch of Jesus' hand has power; this corresponds to the previous story of the cure of the centurion's servant. There the word alone of Jesus is so powerful that it cures from a distance (8:8-13). In contrast, Mark has Jesus take hold of her hand and lift her to her feet. In Matthew, she rises herself.

Finally, what seems like a small concluding detail will have great significance: "She arose and served *him*," not *them* as in Mark. It is thus a personal service to Jesus, not just hospitality to the group. The Greek verb to express this is significant; it is related to *diakonia*, meaning personal service. This word expresses a central theme in Matthew: personal service to Jesus. We have seen the same word in the judgment scene; it appears in the question of those on the left hand: "Lord, when did we see you hungry or thirsty or a stranger or naked or sick or in prison and did not *minister* to you?" (25:44). Later we will take special note that Matthew emphasizes the same *diakonia* in regard to Mary Magdalene and the other women at the foot of the cross (27:55).

The Cure of Jairus' Daughter and of the Woman with the Hemorrhage
Matthew 9:18-26

While he was thus speaking to them, behold, a ruler came in and knelt before him, saying, "My daughter has just died; but come and lay your hand on her, and she will live." And Jesus rose and followed him, with his disciples. And behold, a woman who had suffered from a hemorrhage for twelve years came up behind him and touched the fringe of his garment; for she said to herself, "If I only touch his garment I shall be made well." Jesus turned, and seeing her he said, "Take heart, daughter; your faith has made you well." And instantly the woman was made well. And when Jesus came to the ruler's house, and saw the flute players, and the crowd making a tumult, he said, "Depart; for the girl is not dead but sleeping." And they laughed at him. But when the crowd had been put outside, he went in and took her by the hand, and the girl arose. And the report of this went through all that district.

If we look at chapter 5 of Mark's Gospel in comparison, even a quick glance reveals that Matthew has cut almost two-thirds of Mark's story. In general, details about the audience and the recipients of the cure are missing—for example, the name of Jairus, the age of the daughter, the setting of the miracle. Instead, Matthew highlights the person and authority of the *one who cures*; Mark gives more attention to the *faith of those cured*.

Let us note some significant details in Matthew's account. From the very beginning, attention is focused on Jesus and the worship given him by the unnamed ruler. In Matthew, the child has just died; in Mark, the child was still alive when Jesus was first called. It becomes a clear case of Jesus' power to raise the dead to life. The words "And Jesus *rose* and followed [the ruler], *with his disciples*" hints that Jesus' own resurrection will raise others as well. The words "Lay your hand on her, and she will live" stress the power of Jesus' touch, as we saw in the cure of Peter's mother-in-law.

The same themes continue in the cure of the woman with the hemorrhage. She came up secretly behind Jesus to touch the fringe of his garment. Secrecy was needed because she knew that her uncleanness was so deadly and contagious that a mere touch would transfer it to others (Lev 15:25-30). She said to herself, "If I only touch his garment, I shall be made well" (9:21). Here again Jesus' personal power is stressed. He not only knows that he has been touched but reads the woman's mind as well. The woman is not healed by her touch, as in Mark's Gospel, but by Jesus' initiative and word. He turns, sees her, and says, "Take heart, daughter; your faith has made you well." Only then does Matthew write, "And instantly the woman was made well" (9:22). R. H. Gundry notes, "Only a word, only a touch—such emphasis shows that Jesus' authority is so great that for miraculous cures it needs but little exercise."[31]

Matthew then returns to the story of the ruler's daughter. The previous themes reach a dramatic completion. Jesus' name is repeated a third time for added emphasis (9:23). On his initiative *he comes* to the ruler's house. He takes command of the situation and orders the flute players and the crowd to depart. There is no mention, as in Mark, of Peter, James, and John. Jesus alone encounters the powers of death. He *comes* to the child, takes her by the hand, and the girl herself arises. There is no command or motif of secrecy as in Mark. The report goes out to everyone.

Putting all this together, we see that Matthew emphasizes the authoritative power of Jesus through his word and touch over all the powers of death—a living death, as in the case of the woman with the flow of blood, or a physical death, as in the case of the ruler's daughter. It is Jesus' initiative and action that are essential. The actions of the recipients are in response to his personal intervention. These themes will carry over to the final disclosure and nature of Matthew's hero in the passion accounts.

The Canaanite Woman's Faith (15:21-28)

Contrary to Matthew's usual practice of shortening Mark's accounts of miracles, this one receives equal space. Here we will point out some of the notable elements that prepare for the gradual unveiling of Matthew's hero.

In this story Jesus journeys into the predominantly Gentile district of Tyre and Sidon. In Mark 7:24-30 Jesus was hidden in a house, where the woman somehow finds him. In Matthew, though, everything is in the open. The woman even calls out to Jesus, "Have mercy on me, O Lord, Son of David; my daughter is severely possessed by a demon" (15:22). We are surprised by her confession of faith using the titles "Lord" and "Son of David." She even comes up to Jesus and kneels before him in worship.

In Matthew, the disciples tell Jesus to "send her away, for she is crying after us." Jesus himself then says, "I was sent only to the lost sheep of the house of Israel" (15:23-24). This shows the opposition of the disciples to any kind of Gentile apostolate, and the barrier to it in the divine plan, as shown by Jesus' words "I was only sent. . . ." Yet even in face of these impossible obstacles, the woman persists and exclaims, "Lord, help me" (15:25). Jesus repeats his own limitation with rather harsh words, "It is not fair to take the children's bread and throw it to the dogs." Despite this answer, the woman suggests that even dogs eat of the crumbs that fall from their master's table. Jesus responds, "O woman, great is your faith! Be it done for you as you desire" (15:28).

Jesus' praise of the woman's faith is the greatest given to anyone in the Gospel. It is similar to that given to the centurion, who was told by Jesus, "Amen, I say to you, not even in Israel have I found such faith" (8:10). In view of this faith, Jesus will amend the divine plan and extend the "master's table" (in the woman's words) to the Gentiles as well. This will be shown in the story of the second multiplication of loaves, which immediately follows in 15:32-39. In contrast to what he says to the woman, Jesus speaks elsewhere of the *little* faith of Peter and the disciples (14:31; 16:8). He then cures her daughter from a distance, just as he cured the centurion's servant from a distance (8:13) and as he will "cure" the whole Gentile world through his last commission to the disciples on the Galilean mountain (28:19).

The story of this woman brings out a new element in discipleship, namely, an absolute faith in the person of Jesus despite impossible circumstances, even the opposition of the disciples and the apparent biblical plan of God. It is a faith that the bread of the Jewish Son of David is not only for his own people but for the whole world as well. It is a faith that Jesus can cure from a distance. The audience would understand this as made possible through his death. The woman's story prepares for the passion narrative, where such faith will not be found in Peter and his disciples. They will abandon Jesus at his arrest and his death on the cross. The audience, however, will find a complete example of faith in the actions of the Gospel heroes at that crucial time.

The Unique Characteristics of Matthew's Anointing at Bethany (26:6-13)

To study this incident in detail, we will give the entire text here.

> Now when Jesus was at Bethany in the house of Simon the leper, a woman came up to him with an alabaster jar of very expensive ointment, and she poured it on his head, as he sat at table. But when the disciples saw it, they were indignant, saying, "Why this waste? For this ointment might have been sold for a large sum and given to the poor." But Jesus, aware of this, said to them, "Why do you trouble the woman? For she has done a beautiful thing to me. For you always have the poor with you, but you will not always have me. In pouring this ointment on my body she has done it to prepare me for burial. Amen, I say to you, wherever this gospel is preached in the whole world, what she has done will be told in memory of her."

When we studied this episode in Mark's Gospel (14:3-9), we saw that the story was closely connected with Jesus' last words and testament in chapter 13. Together with the story of the poor widow (12:41-44), it formed a literary frame around Jesus' last discourse. There Jesus spoke of the coming persecution and even death of the disciples and pointed out how this would be a necessary *martyrion,* or testimony, that would make possible the preaching of the gospel to the world and the return of Jesus. Thus Jesus' final amen saying about the poor widow had special significance—she had given everything, her very life, to God. The woman at Bethany, in recognition of Jesus' true identity through his death, broke the alabaster jar and gave herself, "what she could" (Mark 14:8). Consequently, her action as an ideal disciple would make possible the conversion of the Gentiles and would be known all over the world.

However, we have seen that Matthew's Gospel no longer has the same central perspective. He retells the Bethany story with a new emphasis. As a result, the story of the poor widow, who gave her very life, is omitted entirely. Instead, the action of the Bethany woman is closely linked to the central theme of Jesus' last judgment and its concluding amen statements, first in the positive form, "Amen I say to you, as you did it to one of the least of these . . . you did it to me" (25:40), then in the negative form, "As you did it not . . . (25:45).

Matthew links the Bethany story with the last judgment by a small but significant modification. The phrase "to me" or an equivalent is found some twenty times in the judgment scene as applied to personal service, or *diakonia*, in regard to Jesus. In the Bethany account Matthew has Jesus say, "She has done a beautiful thing *to me*" (26:10). Mark 14:6 has the same except for one word—instead of "to me" (*eis eme*), it has "in regard to me" (*en emoi*). Thus Matthew has brought the woman's action in direct correspondence with the central "to me" of the judgment scene. The total significance of this will emerge as we examine the whole Bethany story according to Matthew's version.

First of all, Matthew's version concentrates more on the person of Jesus. His actual name and not the personal pronoun, as in Mark, opens the story. The woman "comes up to him" (26:7). Mark's description of the breaking of the jar or the giving of "what she had" is omitted. This is because these pointed more to the woman's self-giving, even unto death, in imitation of Jesus. Matthew mentions specifically the indignation of the disciples. Jesus, with his majestic power, is "aware of this" (28:10). The disciples' opposition is exemplified in Judas, who wants to sell Jesus for a (small) price in the next incident (26:14-16), in ironical contrast to their concern over the great price of the ointment that the woman pours on Jesus.

In addition, in Mark's story the woman's action was prophetic. She knew that Jesus was a Messiah ready to suffer and die. So Jesus says, "She has anointed my body beforehand for burying" (14:8). The "beforehand" is omitted by Matthew, who does not have a follow up with the women going to anoint Jesus at the tomb; instead they go to see the sepulchre (28:1).

Consequently, Matthew does not have the woman anoint Jesus in recognition of his coming death but as a kind service that has meaning within the story itself. Jesus recognizes that it will supply for the missing anointment at his burial, but that is not the woman's intention.

The pivotal phrase of Matthew's story is found in the words "She has done a beautiful thing to me" (26:10). A more literal translation of the Greek *ergon* would be "deed" or "work" instead of "thing." To highlight this word, Matthew places it at the beginning of his sentence (*ergon gar kalon*) instead of in the second place (*kalon ergon*), as Mark does. Matthew does this because the word is very important in his Gospel. He constantly uses the word "do" in regard to action—about eighty-five times. This culminates with Jesus' final testament: "As you did it to one of the least of these . . . you did it to me" (25:40).

For Matthew, the essence of the woman's action is that brought out by Jesus' word that it was done "to me." This establishes the link to Jesus' last testament in the preceding scene of the final judgment (25:31-46). The woman's loving service to Jesus becomes a model for Christian action. We use the term "loving service" because the last judgment scene does not envision mere external works of kindness. They are called a *diakonia*, a noun derived from the verb used when those on the left hand complain to the judge, "Lord, when did we see you hungry or thirsty or a stranger or naked or sick or in prison, and did not *minister* to you?" (25:44). This personal element is stressed in the story of the anointing at Bethany, where the simple action of loving service is contrasted with the large amount of money that could be given to the poor if the ointment were sold.

The solemn amen saying of Jesus at the end of the story has a special Matthean emphasis. In Mark we saw that the symbolic offering of the woman's life represents the total sacrifice of the persecuted believer that will be the necessary witness to all the world. Thus the woman's deed will be told "wherever the gospel is preached in the whole world'' (14:9). Matthew makes a significant change. Jesus says, ''Wherever *this* gospel [instead of *the* gospel] is preached.'' Matthew also makes a corresponding change in Jesus' last testament (Mark 13:10; Matt 24:14). With this distinction the author may be telling his audience that *this* gospel is his own gospel, one that emphasizes good deeds that are done to others as to Christ himself. The Bethany woman is a supreme example of this in her personal, loving service to the Master.

The Only Ones Who Follow Jesus as Far as the Cross

As in the Gospel of Mark, Mary Magdalene and the other women are the essential and only witnesses of Jesus' death, his burial, and the empty tomb. All Jesus' male disciples had fled at his arrest. Peter had even publicly denied that he knew his Master. In Galilee, Jesus had called his disciples and asked them to follow him so that he could make them fishers of human beings like himself (3:19). Like Mark, Matthew notes that the women ''had followed him from Galilee'' (27:55), the only ones to do so as far as the cross. Also, Mary Magdalene merits the title of being the principal hidden hero of the Gospel because she is named three times, and always first (27:56, 61; 28:1). This is even more forceful in Matthew than in Mark, for the second and third mention of the women in Matthew have only Mary Magdalene and ''the other Mary.'' This seems to play down the importance of the second woman; she remains anonymous and may be there only as a companion of Mary Magdalene.

Matthew's passion account differs significantly from Mark's, and his description of the ideal disciple has some notable changes and new aspects. First of all, he writes as follows about the women by the cross: ''There were also many women there, looking on from afar, who had followed Jesus from Galilee, *ministering* to him; among whom were Mary Magdalene, and Mary the mother of James and Joseph, and the mother of the sons of Zebedee'' (27:55-56). The word ''ministering" deserves special emphasis because Matthew gives it special attention by moving it from the following sentence (as in Mark) and placing it along with the verb "had followed." Thus Matthew continues the stress on personal service to Jesus, a theme he began with his description of the first woman cured in the Gospel—Peter's mother-in-law. There Matthew wrote that she "served *him* [Jesus]." We have seen how this personal emphasis continued through the Gospel and culminated in the last judgment scene. This in turn was followed by a practical example in the anointing at Bethany.

This *diakonia* receives further attention in the closing section of the Gospel. After Jesus' burial, Matthew writes, "Mary Magdalene and the other Mary were there, sitting opposite the sepulchre" (27:61). Their attitude is one of vigilant waiting, something that Matthew has Jesus often stress in his last testament (24:42, 45-51; 25:13, 14-30). In Matthew this prayerful waiting takes on the aspect of a personal service to Jesus. This is shown in Jesus' prayer in the garden, where he says to his disciples, "Remain here, and watch *with me*" (26:38). The phrase "with me" is a personal reference—keeping vigil with Christ—not found in Mark. In Matthew's garden scene, Jesus' sorrow seems to be more over the failure of his disciples than over the prospect of his death. Thus he repeats to Peter, "Could you not watch *with me* one hour" (26:40). In view of this, the actions of the women, especially Mary Magdalene, take on added significance in contrast to the failure of the disciples, especially Peter.

The women's vigil is interrupted by sunset and the arrival of the sabbath, but it continues again when the two women return to the tomb: "Now after the sabbath, toward the dawn of the first day of the week, Mary Magdalene and the other Mary went to see the sepulchre" (28:1). The women return not to anoint Jesus' body, as in Mark and Luke, but to continue their prayerful waiting for his resurrection. This is a special quality of the Gospel heroes that Matthew wants his audience to imitate. Their waiting is dramatically rewarded. An earthquake occurs and an angel rolls back the huge stone from the tomb entrance. The angel announces to them that Jesus is not there but has risen "as he said" (28:6). These last words, which are given only in Matthew, bring out the basis for the women's vigil. They trusted in Jesus and his words even after the shattering experience of the cross.

The next surprise for the women is the commission that the angel of God entrusts to them: they are to be the first heralds of the resurrection to the world. The angel tells them, "Go quickly and tell his disciples that he has risen from the dead, and behold, he is going before you to Galilee; there you will see him" (28:7). Mark had only the message about Jesus' going before them into Galilee, but Matthew adds the fact that "he has risen from the dead." This places added emphasis on Mary Magdalene and her companion as the first ones to announce Jesus' resurrection. The women faithfully and promptly obey the angel's word: "they departed quickly from the tomb with fear and great joy, and ran to tell his disciples" (28:8).

Mark's version of the women's departure is remarkably different: "They went out and fled from the tomb; for trembling and astonishment had come upon them; and they said nothing to any one, for they were afraid" (16:8). The trembling, flight, and silence in Mark's ending changes into fear and great joy in Matthew as the women run to tell the disciples. Matthew thus presents his Gospel hero as an example of faithfulness and prompt, joyful obedience to God's word through the angel.

The final outcome of the women's waiting, trust, and prayer comes in a surprise encounter with the risen Jesus. The women become the first ones to actually see the risen Jesus. This earns for them the title "apostles," meaning those who actually saw the risen Lord. Paul called himself an apostle because he had seen the risen Lord: "Am I not an apostle? Have I not seen Jesus our Lord?" (1 Cor 9:1). Matthew describes Jesus' apparition to the women as follows: "And behold, Jesus met them and said, 'Hail!' And they came up and took hold of his feet and worshiped him. Then Jesus said to them, 'Do not be afraid; go and tell my brethren to go to Galilee, and there they will see me' '' (28:10).

In typical fashion, the author describes the initiative of the risen Jesus in coming to the women and greeting them. They respond with what appears to be divine worship, if we bear in mind Jesus' majestic title as Son of God made possible by his victorious death and resurrection. It also parallels the disciples' worship in the final mountain scene, in which Jesus announces that he has all power and authority in heaven as on earth (28:18). Now the women receive their apostolic commission directly from the risen Jesus as he personally tells them to announce to "his brethren" that he is going before them into Galilee. The word "brethren" reflects the family emphasis in Matthew's Gospel. Jesus, the women, and the Twelve become Jesus' new family, distinguished by mutual personal, loving service.

Matthew carefully notes that the women fulfilled Jesus' word by introducing the next section with the words "While they were going . . ." (28:11). He may be doing this to contrast the women's faithfulness with the lack of faith and deception of the Jewish chief priests and Pharisees, who instructed the soldiers to go out also but to spread the false story that the disciples stole Jesus' body while the guards were asleep.

The obedience and personal dedication to Christ shown by Mary Magdalene and her companion make the Gospel's conclusion possible. They faithfully tell the disciples to gather in Galilee. There the final mountain theophany and the commissioning of the disciples to make disciples of all nations take place. Thus these women deserve the title "apostles to the apostles."

Summary

Matthew composed his Gospel to meet the needs of an audience facing a crisis in regard to their relationship with Judaism. To help wavering Christians, the author presents a unique understanding of Jesus' person as well as his teachings. The death of Jesus is a great reversal from defeat to victory because of the divine plan. From obedient Son, Jesus becomes the powerful and authoritative Son of God. In view of this, the whole Gospel emphasizes Jesus' person and his powerful teaching word. The ideal disciple follows these words as found in Matthew's five great discourses, especially the Sermon on the Mount.

The whole Gospel moves toward the final mountain scene and Christophany, in which Jesus as powerful Son of God hands over his teachings to his disciples and commissions them to go out to the whole world. He guarantees that he will always be present with them. One important way the ideal disciple will find this presence will be through an encounter with Jesus by loving service to the poor, the hungry, and the needy. This is brought out in the final judgment scene by the words of Jesus' last testament: "Amen, I say to you, as you did it to one of the least of these . . . you did it to me" (25:40).

The ideal disciple, as embodied in the Gospel hero, follows and imitates Jesus as far as the cross. She is distinguished by a personal ministry to Jesus in the person of the poor and afflicted. This *diakonia* also takes place through vigilant prayer, worship, and obedience to the risen Jesus. In this way the gospel message will reach the whole world as people become deeply moved and impressed by the living example of Jesus' disciples. The hidden Gospel hero, who is principally Mary Magdalene, is the true counterpart of Jesus in the Gospel of Matthew.

CHAPTER THREE

THE GOSPEL OF LUKE

The last to remain, the first to return and remember

The Gospel of Luke cannot be studied alone. It is part of a two-volume work, the Gospel and the Acts of the Apostles. Like the other evangelists, Luke also uses dramatic narrative, but he has a "double feature," with close literary and exegetical links between his two volumes. Modern scholarship has increasingly brought out the need to study both books as a unified whole.[32] Luke himself reminds his audience of this as he begins the Acts of the Apostles with the words: "In the first book, O Theophilus, I have dealt with all that Jesus began to do and teach, until the day when he was taken up . . ." (Acts 1:1-2). Luke's second book then starts with this point and continues on as Jesus' apostles, with the presence and power of the Holy Spirit, take the good news to the whole world.

The Gospel of Luke as a "Gospel of Women"

At first glance, Luke's Gospel indeed appears to be a "Gospel of Women" in comparison with other New Testament documents. The following women in Luke's Gospel appeared nowhere in Mark and Matthew: Elizabeth, the mother of John the Baptist and a model of faith; Anna, a prophetess, who appears in the Temple at Jesus' presentation (Luke 2:36-38); Joanna and Susanna, traveling companions of Jesus, along with Mary Magdalene (Luke 8:2-3); Mary and Martha, the two sisters who provide Jesus with hospitality and listen to his word (Luke 10:38-42). Mary, the mother of Jesus, is indeed mentioned in Mark and Matthew; however, only in Luke does she appear as a real *person*. She is portrayed as a model for believers with the words "Blessed is she who believed . . ." (Luke 1:45).

In addition to this, women appear in stories and parables found nowhere else. In Jesus' greatest miracle he raises up from the dead the only son of the widow of Nain (Luke 7:11-17). We have a long story about the anointing of Jesus' feet by a sinner in a Pharisee's home (Luke 7:36-50). This story contains details from Mark's account of the anointing at Bethany, a story that Luke omits from its usual place before the passion. There is also the cure of a woman on the sabbath (Luke 13:10-17). Finally, there are special parables about women: the parable of the lost coin (Luke 15:8-10) and the parable of the persistent widow and the unjust judge (Luke 18:1-8).

Luke's second volume, the Acts of the Apostles, singles out women who played key roles in the early Church. There is Mary, the mother of Mark (Acts 12:12), whose house in Jerusalem was an important center for early Christians. Peter returned there after his arrest and found a group of believers gathered together in "earnest prayer for him" (Acts 12:5, 12).

The spread of the gospel to Europe was made possible by a group of women who listened to Paul's preaching by a river outside Philippi. A prominent and rich woman among them, Lydia, listened to Paul's word, became a convert, and made her household into a Christian center (Acts 16:13-15). In Corinth, a Christian couple from Rome named Aquila and Priscilla welcomed Paul into their home, which became a center for Paul's apostolate (Acts 18:1-4). Priscilla seems to have been the more active partner, since she is usually mentioned first. This couple was so important for Paul that he brought them to Ephesus, where he left them to begin a new apostolate while he journeyed to Jerusalem (Acts 18:18-21). In Ephesus they converted Apollos, a gifted preacher and former disciple of John the Baptist (Acts 18:24-28).

Shattering the Illusion of the "Gospel of Women"

We would expect the Gospel of Luke to present a superlative picture of our hidden Gospel hero, but instead we will be greatly disappointed. We will begin by noting the differences between Luke's Gospel and those of Mark and Matthew, and then we will examine the reasons behind Luke's changes in view of his purpose.

First of all, we saw in Matthew and Mark that the ideal disciple is one who follows Jesus from Galilee all the way to the cross. Mary Magdalene and the other women filled this description perfectly. Jesus had said to his disciples in Galilee, after John's arrest and the prospect of his own: "Follow me and I will make you become fishers of human beings" (Mark 1:17; Matt 4:19). The two Gospels then note that "they followed him." This formed a distinct and meaningful parallel to the scene at Jesus' death, in which Mary and the others "followed him" (Mark 15:41; Matt 27:55).

However, if we examine Luke's Gospel carefully, we will find that this key correspondence almost entirely disappears. Jesus' first call in Galilee centers around Simon Peter. Jesus gets into his boat, teaches the people, and then tells Simon Peter to let down his nets for a catch. Despite the fact that the disciples have toiled all night and caught nothing, Peter says, "At your word I will let down the nets" (Luke 5:5). Following Jesus' word, Simon Peter lets down the nets and encloses a great multitude of fish. He then acknowledges his own sinfulness and is completely astonished at the miraculous catch of fish. Then Jesus says to *Simon Peter*, "Do not be afraid; henceforth you will be catching human beings" (Luke 5:11). Only after this does the story mention that Simon Peter, James, and John "left everything and followed him." Later we will see that Luke's emphasis on the Twelve, especially Peter, will be a principal cause for diminishing the stature of the female Gospel heroes.

The next significant difference occurs in Luke's description of Jesus' traveling companions: "And the twelve were with him, and also some women who had been healed of evil spirits and infirmities: Mary, called Magdalene, from whom seven demons had gone out, and Joanna, the wife of Chuza, Herod's steward, and Susanna, and many others, who provided for them [or 'him' in some manuscripts] out of their means'' (Luke 8:1-3). This text reveals some features of these women. First of all, they were persons whom Jesus had cured in some way. The exorcisms mentioned and the ancient connection between disease and wrongdoing suggest that the women were guilty of some grave sin(s). The description of Mary Magdalene as one from whom seven demons had gone out hints that she was a very lively sinner at that! The role of these women seems to have been principally one of caring for the material needs of Jesus and the apostles from their own personal means.

The most significant differences occur in Luke's passion and resurrection accounts. We saw in Matthew and Mark that Mary Magdalene and her companions were the only witnesses of Jesus' death, burial, and the empty tomb. In Matthew they were the first ones to see the risen Jesus. This was in contrast to the disciples, who fled at Jesus' arrest, and Peter, who denied that he even knew the Master. All this changes in Luke's Gospel, where many others are present at Jesus' death: "And all his acquaintances and the women who had followed him from Galilee stood at a distance and saw these things" (Luke 23:49). Luke adds "all his acquaintances," literally "those known by him." He can write this because he has no reference to the disciples' running away after Jesus' arrest. He does have the denial of Peter, but this resulted in almost instant pardon when "the Lord turned and looked at Peter" (Luke 22:61). This pardon had already been "guaranteed" at the Last Supper when Jesus stated that Satan had desired to sift the disciples like wheat. However, Jesus had prayed for Peter, that once he turned back he would confirm the others (Luke 22:31-32).

We saw in Matthew and Mark that the women's names were announced three times to the audience to emphasize their importance, especially Mary Magdalene. Here in Luke 23:49 and again in 23:54 they are unnamed. Anonymously they come to anoint Jesus' body (Luke 24:1). Luke furnishes their names only at the end when he notes that Mary Magdalene and the others were among those who told the apostles about the empty tomb and the vision of angels. These angels give no commission to the women, as they do in Mark and Matthew. Finally, when Mary and the others give the news to the apostles, their reaction is disbelief, with even a hint of disparagement: "These words seemed to them an idle tale, and they did not believe them" (Luke 24:11). Even the way the story is told does not single out Mary Magdalene. She seems to be part of a considerable delegation of women: "Now it was Mary Magdalene and Joanna and Mary the mother of James and the other women with them who told this to the apostles" (Luke 24:10).

Luke, therefore, does not describe the women as the real heralds of the resurrection to the world. They receive no commission from the angels, nor do they see the risen Jesus and receive a message from him, as in Matthew. Even on receiving the news from the women, the disciples reject their testimony. Instead, Luke builds his case on direct apparitions of the risen Jesus to Simon Peter (Luke 24:34), to the disciples on the way to Emmaus (Luke 24:30), and to the Eleven gathered at table (Luke 24:36-40).[33] It seems to be even emphasized that the women did not see the risen Jesus. In addition, Luke omits the unique preparatory story of the anointing at Bethany, which is connected to the women's action by the cross in Matthew and Mark. Two of the disciples leave Jerusalem on Sunday morning and seem to take little account of the women's experience. On their way they say to Jesus, disguised as a stranger: "We had hoped that he [Jesus] was the one to redeem Israel. Yes, and besides all this, it is now the third day since this happened. Moreover, some women of our company amazed us. They were at the tomb early in the morning and did not find his body; and they came back saying that they

had even seen a vision of angels, who said that he was alive"
(Luke 24:21-23).

Luke's Reason for Downstaging the Women

Luke's reasons only become evident in light of the purposes
of his Gospel. Some of these are outlined at the very beginning. He writes to a certain Theophilus about "the things
which have been accomplished among us" (Luke 1:1). Luke
wants Theophilus to know the truth (or certainty) of the things
of which he has been taught or informed (Luke 1:4). If Luke
wanted to give Theophilus added certainty, there must have
been some things about which he was doubtful or uncertain.

Luke does not give us an explicit list of these questions, but
there are indications in his Gospel and the Acts of the Apostles
that he was very concerned about errors and increased diver-
sity among Christians. In fact, Luke has the Apostle Paul, in
a kind of last testament, summon the presbyters of Ephesus
for a final instruction before he goes on to Jerusalem and probably death. Paul tells them, "I know that after my departure
fierce wolves will come in among you, not sparing the flock;
and from among your own selves will arise men speaking per-
verse things, to draw away the disciples after them" (Acts
20:29-30).

Some of these errors, by way of illustration, concerned the
reality of Jesus' bodily existence, especially after his resurrection, when Christians experienced his presence in the breaking of bread. These teachings probably had their source in
Gnostic tendencies.[34] We find examples of these questions in
the story of the risen Jesus' first apparition to all the disciples
at table. After Jesus' greeting, Luke writes, "They were startled
and frightened, and supposed that they saw a spirit. And he
said to them, 'Why are you troubled, and why do question-
ings rise in your hearts? See my hands and my feet, that it is
I myself; handle me, and see; for a spirit has not flesh and
bones as you see that I have.' . . . And while they still dis-
believed for joy, and wondered, he said to them, 'Have you

anything here to eat?' They gave him a piece of broiled fish, and he took it and ate before them'' (Luke 24:37-43).

Luke no doubt relates this incident for the benefit of his own audience, to give them the certainty mentioned in the beginning of his gospel (Luke 1:4). To have this certainty, the audience must have an authoritative tradition about the breaking of the bread (as well as other matters). That is why Luke stresses the special opening call of Peter. He is the one who will become Jesus' special successor in his mission to save people.

Luke, therefore, places special emphasis on Peter and the Twelve in regard to teachings about Jesus' new bread. For example, in the account of the multiplication of loaves, the apostles' role is given much more attention than in the other Gospels. Before the miracle of the loaves, Jesus called the Twelve together and gave them power and authority over demons and diseases as well as a commission to preach the kingdom of God and to heal (Luke 9:1). Upon their return, ''the apostles told him [Jesus] what they had done'' (Luke 9:10). They then took the initiative to ask Jesus to feed and care for the crowds: ''The twelve came and said to him, 'Send the crowd away, to go into the villages and country round about, to lodge and get provisions' '' (Luke 9:12).

The emphasis on Peter and the Twelve is even more marked in Luke's Last Supper account as compared with that in Matthew and Mark. Jesus sends *Peter and John* to make preparations for the final Passover (Luke 22:8). Later, Luke writes, ''When the hour came, he sat at table, and the apostles with him'' (Luke 22:14). Jesus promises them that they will preside over his banquet table in the coming kingdom as his successors: ''As my Father appointed a kingdom for me, so do I appoint for you that you may eat and drink at my table in my kingdom, and sit on thrones judging the twelve tribes of Israel'' (Luke 22:28-30). At this Last Supper, Jesus prays especially for Simon that he may turn to him after failure and confirm the rest (Luke 22:31-34).

The same pattern continues in the resurrection accounts. Luke ends his Gospel with appearances of Jesus to the disciples gathered at table to emphasize the fulfillment of Jesus' promise at the Last Supper to eat with him in the kingdom. The appearance of Jesus to the disciples at Emmaus during a meal is the first one related by Luke. This means that the appearance to the women, as told in Matthew, is omitted. When the disciples of Emmaus return to Jerusalem, they are told: "The Lord has risen indeed, and has appeared to Simon!" (Luke 24:34). Then Jesus appears again at table to the assembled disciples and assures them of the reality of his presence (Luke 24:36). Finally, he explains to them the Scriptures and gives them his last commission to carry his good news to the world (24:44-49).

The apostolic witness is confirmed in Jesus' last words: "You are witnesses of these things" (Luke 24:48). We have seen the consequences of this: The primary witness and commissioning of the women that was so important in Matthew and Mark have been put aside to emphasize the position, authority, and witness of Peter and the Twelve.

The same preeminence of Peter and the Twelve, especially about the meaning of the breaking of bread, continues in the Acts of the Apostles. Luke carefully gives all their names again at the beginning of his second volume in order to emphasize continuity and succession (Acts 1:13-14). There is even an election of a new twelfth member, perhaps to make sure that no one unauthorized would claim that title (Acts 1:15-26). When the Jerusalem Christians broke bread together, they shared not only bread but also "the apostles' teachings" (Acts 2:42). When Peter spoke to Cornelius and his assembled friends, he emphasized that he was a chosen witness of the resurrection and of the risen Jesus' meals with the apostles: "God raised him on the third day and made him manifest; not to all the people but to us who were chosen by God as witnesses, who ate and drank with him after he rose from the dead" (Acts 10:40-41).

There is no doubt, then, that Luke wants to emphasize the special place of Peter, and secondarily that of the other apostles, in regard to the meaning of bread and Jesus' real presence with them after his resurrection. This means that other witnesses, such as the women, must be put in second place or simply omitted. This accounts for the striking difference in Luke's presentation of these Gospel heroes in his closing chapters. He will, however, ascribe to these women another unusual and inner role that is not found in Matthew and Mark. This will be the subject of our next section.

The Last to Remain, the First to Return and Remember

The women who had come with him [Jesus] from Galilee followed, and saw the tomb, and how *his body* was laid; then they returned, and prepared spices and ointments (Luke 23:56).
But on the first day of the week, at early dawn, they went to the tomb, taking the spices which they had prepared. And they found the stone rolled away from the tomb, but when they went in they did not find the *body* ["of the Lord Jesus" in some manuscripts] (Luke 24:1-3).
They were at the tomb early in the morning and did not find his *body* . . . (Luke 24:22-23).

In each of these texts we have italicized the reference to the body of Jesus. Only Luke has this emphasis on Jesus' body in connection with Mary Magdalene and the women. In the previous section we saw Luke's concern for his audience in regard to the bodily reality of Jesus in order to counteract the docetic tendencies of some Christians. That is why the testimony of the "last to remain" is so important for Luke and his audience.

In the first text above, it is the women who actually see the dead body of Jesus placed in the tomb and note how it was laid. They do so because they want to return and offer their last act of devotion to Jesus by anointing his body. In the second text, they actually do return for this purpose and find the body missing. In the third text, the disciples on the way to Emmaus note that the women did not find his body, despite the fact that they saw him buried, noted carefully where his body was, how it was placed, and then returned after the sabbath to anoint it. Thus, Luke has Mary Magdalene and the other women provide this unique witness of the death of Jesus and his human, bodily reality. In doing so, the author selects them, especially Mary Magdalene, for an essential role in providing testimony in such an essential matter.

> "Why do you seek the living among the dead? He is not here, ['but has risen' in some texts]. *Remember* how he told you, while he was still in Galilee, that the Son of man must be delivered into the hands of sinful men, and be crucified, and on the third day rise." And they *remembered* his words, and returning from the tomb they told all this to the eleven and to all the rest. Now it was Mary Magdalene and Joanna and Mary the mother of James and the other women with them who told this to the apostles (Luke 24:5-10).

A key Lukan theme is this remembering. To grasp its importance, we must discover how it fits into the central purposes of the Gospel. If it is a key factor, then the women, especially Mary Magdalene, have heroes' roles as the first to remember Jesus' words.

In regard to Luke's purposes in this motif of remembering, we turn again to the opening statement of his Gospel. In the very first verse he is concerned about "the things which have been accomplished among us." This undoubtedly refers to God's plan for salvation in the Scriptures. At the end of his introduction, Luke tells Theophilus that he wants him to know the truth or have certainty about the things he has been taught (Luke 1:4). Once again, there must have been areas of great difficulty or uncertainty if Luke made that observation. What were these uncertainties? We have already discussed one area, the reality of Jesus' bodily existence, especially in his resurrection body.

Another important question would be how the divine plan in the Scriptures could have been fulfilled by Jesus. To all appearances, Jesus died on the cross as a disgraceful failure. How could such a tragic ending be according to God's plan in the Scriptures? And if it was, who had the ability and the authority to interpret it? The Scriptures as a whole envisioned a glorious and triumphant Messiah who could save Israel by his power. A model for this was their great leader Moses, who saved them by being a strong military and political leader. But Theophilus had been taught about a weak and powerless Messiah who died on a cross and was the laughingstock of his opponents and even of intellectual Greeks. Could a Messiah unable to even save himself be one who could save others? Such a matter would be extremely important for Christians, not only in response to pagans but in regard to their own suffering, persecution, and even possible death because of their faith. Was this something valuable and meaningful as part of the divine plan?

We can best find Luke's viewpoint and answer to these vital questions by going to his scene at the cross, which could be entitled "The Christ Who Could Not Even Save Himself!"[35] There Luke presents Theophilus and his audience with a poignant description of the triple temptation Jesus faced in his dying moments. The first temptation is from the rulers of the people:

> The rulers scoffed at him, saying, "He saved others; let him save himself, if he is the Christ of God, his Chosen One!" (Luke 23:35).

The second temptation comes from the soldiers who crucified him:

> The soldiers also mocked him, coming up and offering him vinegar, and saying, "If you are the King of the Jews, save yourself!" (Luke 23:36-37).

The third temptation is from one of the criminals crucified at his side:

> One of the criminals who were hanged railed at him, saying, "Are you not the Christ? Save yourself and us!" (Luke 23:39).

All three temptations have common themes: First, there is the title "Christ" (from Jews) or "King" (from Gentiles). Second, in all three Jesus is mocked because he is unable to save himself, and in the third case, to save others as well.

This desperate scene at the cross makes it surprising that one of the crucified ones would call on Jesus for help and be promised salvation that very day. This would provide the audience with a basis for accepting the disgrace and failure of the cross as a means and instrument of salvation. Luke makes the paradox even stronger by calling the "good thief" not a thief at all but a criminal, changing the word used by Matthew and Mark. This is done to show that any person, no matter how desperate the situation he or she was in, could call upon Christ as he did, and that the one who "could not save others" really could do so in a hidden and mysterious way.

The above three temptations have a special diabolical air about them as a direct counterpart to the triple temptation by the devil after Jesus' baptism. There the temptation of Jesus was likewise to save himself from dying of hunger after forty days of fasting. Then, too, the third temptation to throw himself down from the Temple and trust God to save him from death is similar to the temptation to come down from the cross. The fact that the third temptation of the devil takes place (in a vision) in Jerusalem makes the parallel to the cross even stronger. Luke concludes Jesus' temptations by noting that the devil would return (Luke 4:13). He does so by entering Judas for betrayal (Luke 22:3), in shaking Peter and the disciples (Luke 22:31), in the power of darkness at Jesus' arrest (Luke 22:53), and finally on the cross.

But why *could* not the Christ save himself? This was a puzzle for Luke's audience. They knew there was no question about Jesus' actual power to do so. They had listened to so many great miracles in the Gospel. For example, Jesus had raised the dead son of a widow (Luke 7:11-17); he had saved his own life when the crowds threatened to push him off the cliff at Nazareth (Luke 4:28-30) or when Herod tried to kill him (Luke

13:31-33). Luke knew that it was essential for his audience to realize that Jesus' death was not a terrible disaster, a satanic victory, or the just punishment of a criminal by Rome.

To help his audience realize this, the evangelist takes great pains to show that Christ's inability was not due to a physical lack of power; it was only because he was "unable" to save himself by his own choice. This choice was to obey a mysterious plan of God in the Scriptures that called for such a seemingly tragic death. Only the divine plan could make it the surprising means to save others that would turn all the world's plans upside down. Luke's audience must have experienced the mockery and laughter of Greeks whenever they admitted that they worshiped a crucified and helpless Messiah. An example of this was the Athenians' mockery after Paul spoke of a man risen from the dead (Acts 17:31-32). Paul also described the preaching of a crucified Christ as a folly to the Gentiles and a stumbling block to Jews (1 Cor 1:23).

To answer his audience's needs, Luke presents the dominant Gospel theme of God's hidden plan to save through a helpless Messiah. He does this especially through Jesus' triple prediction about his coming suffering and death, which is followed by instructions on discipleship. We have already seen this triple schema in Matthew and Mark. However, Luke has a unique feature not found in the others. In Matthew and Mark the predictions are indeed difficult sayings, but in Luke they are completely hidden and incapable of being understood, because Luke wants to show that only Jesus could know the secret divine plan to bring about salvation through the human failure and disgrace of the cross. Then after his death only the risen Jesus can reveal this to others.

Jesus' first prediction is in Luke 9:22 and is very similar to that in Mark 8:31. Luke, however, omits Peter's objection and Jesus' reprimand, because he knows that Jesus' predictions concern scriptures hidden in God's plan that his disciples could not possibly have discovered. This becomes evident in the second prediction, in which Jesus adds, "Let these words sink

into your ears; for the Son of man is to be delivered into the
hands of men" (Luke 9:44). Luke then writes, "But they did
not understand this saying, and it was concealed from them,
that they should not perceive it; and they were afraid to ask
him about this saying" (Luke 9:45). In contrast, Mark says only,
"They did not understand the saying, and they were afraid
to ask him" (9:32). Luke's phrase "it was concealed from
them" shows that it was God's plan to have it hidden. The
same theme is found at the end of the third Lukan prediction:
"They understood none of these things; this saying was hid
from them, and they did not grasp what was said" (18:34).

What were these mysterious scriptures in which God's plan
was concealed? In the Gospel Luke provides the only hint
when Jesus predicts that his disciples will obtain swords and
thus appear to be transgressors. Jesus says: "For I tell you that
this scripture must be fulfilled in me, 'And he was reckoned
with transgressors.' " This text is from Isaiah 53:12, part of a
series of descriptions of a suffering servant of God in exile who
dies at the hands of others. However, his voluntary and obedient death becomes like a temple sacrifice showering bless-
ings and justification on others (Isa 53:4ff.).

Luke's knowledge of these scriptures as a basis for a theology of the cross is confirmed by their appearance in his story
of Philip's conversion of the Ethiopian official in Acts 8:26-40.
As he was returning to Ethiopia in his chariot, this official was
reading one of the above passages in Isaiah about God's suffering servant: "As a sheep led to the slaughter or a lamb before
its shearer is dumb, so he opens not his mouth. In his humili-
ation justice was denied him. Who can describe his generation? For his life is taken up from the earth" (Acts 8:32-33; see
Isa 53:7-8).

Philip began with these scriptures in explaining to the Ethiopian the message about Jesus. As a result, the official asked
to be baptized. It is suggested in this story that only Philip,
moved by the Spirit (Acts 8:29), could know such a hidden
meaning of the scriptures, for he said to the official, "Do you

understand what you are reading?'' He replied, ''How can I, unless some one guides me'' (Acts 8:31).

As a parallel to Philip's explanation, only the risen Christ in the form of a mysterious stranger can enlighten the disciples on the way to Emmaus about the meaning of the scriptures pointing to the suffering and death of Christ. Jesus said to them, '' 'Was it not necessary that the Christ should suffer these things and enter into his glory?' And beginning with Moses and all the prophets, he interpreted to them in all the Scriptures the things concerning himself'' (Luke 24:26-27). Recalling the incident later, the two disciples remarked, ''Did not our hearts burn within us while he talked to us on the road, while he opened to us the scriptures?'' (Luke 24:32).

A final reminder about the scriptures comes during Jesus' last apparition to the Eleven and others at table. Luke writes, ''Then he opened their minds to understand the scriptures, and said to them, 'Thus it is written, that the Christ should suffer and on the third day rise from the dead' '' (Luke 24:45-46).

Luke also underlines the essential place of the scriptural divine plan in his version of the centurion's final acclamation after Jesus' death: ''Now when the centurion saw what had taken place, he praised God, and said, 'Certainly this man was innocent!' '' (Luke 23:47). While the Greek *dikaios* literally means ''just,'' the Revised Standard Version uses ''innocent.'' That is certainly part of the meaning, for Jesus' innocence has been emphasized in the preceding trials and in the declaration of innocence made by the repentant criminal crucified with him. However, there are strong indications that the word means primarily ''just,'' in the sense of doing all that God wants.[36] In this case, it is the fulfillment of God's plan in the Scriptures. The centurion used the word *dikaios* because it had a specific meaning that would include innocence but go much beyond it. Luke uses the word to describe those who do what God wants of them, e.g., Zechariah and Elizabeth, the parents of the Baptist (Luke 1:5); the elderly Simeon (Luke 2:25); those worthy of the resurrection (Luke 14:14); Cornelius, the Roman centurion (Acts 10:22).

The scene at the cross also strengthens this meaning. The centurion's words come right after Jesus' last words, which are a prayer to God, "Father, into your hands I commit my spirit" (Luke 23:46). These words parallel the very first words of Jesus in Luke's Gospel, expressing his total concern to do what his Father wants: literally, "I must be about the things of my Father" (Luke 2:49). The centurion witnessed Jesus die as a faithful Son, doing all that the Father wanted of him. In addition, the fact that Jesus was quoting Scripture (Psalm 31:5) while dying points to the Scriptures as the key area of his obedience. This interpretation of "just man" would be a fitting climax to Luke's presentation of Jesus' death as fulfilling the mysterious plan of God in the Scriptures.

With this background we can now discover how Luke presents the key role of Mary Magdalene and the other women. They are the first to remember Jesus' words when he spoke about his coming suffering and death in the divine plan (Luke 9:22). This remembering occurred when they came to Jesus' tomb on Easter morning and found it empty. They were thoroughly perplexed about this, but the two men standing by in dazzling garments told them that Jesus was not there but alive. The men then reminded the women, "Remember how he told you, while he was still in Galilee, that the Son of man must be delivered into the hands of sinful people, and be crucified, and on the third day rise" (Luke 24:6-7).

Then Luke adds the very significant note, "And they remembered his words, and returning from the tomb they told all this to the eleven and to all the rest." The women, especially Mary Magdalene, are thus singled out as the first to remember Jesus' mysterious prediction about his coming death in view of God's plan in the Scriptures (Luke 9:22-23). That may be the reason why Luke is careful to place their actual names in the Gospel as fellow travelers with Jesus (Luke 8:2-3) *before* Jesus makes the first prediction of his death to his disciples (Luke 9:23). It also explains why Luke is so anxious to describe the ideal disciple, especially a woman, as one who listens to Jesus' word. In the story of Martha and Mary, Mary earns special praise because she "sat at the Lord's feet and listened to his teaching" (Luke 10:39). This listening attitude will also be central in Luke's description of Mary, the mother of Jesus, to whom we will devote a special section.

To sum up: Luke's audience faced the serious problem of a Christ who could not help himself. Luke answers that he could not help himself, although it was within his power, because it was contrary to a hidden divine plan to make the helpless Christ on the cross become God's saving power for the world by reversing all human expectations.

Luke's second volume, the Acts of the Apostles, confirms this key divine scriptural plan. On Pentecost day Peter declares that Jesus' death is "according to the definite plan and foreknowledge of God" (Acts 2:23). Also, he later preaches in the Temple, "What God foretold by the mouth of all the prophets, that his Christ should suffer" (Acts 3:18; see also Acts 4:28). Paul repeats the same teaching in the synagogues of Antioch of Pisidia and Thessalonica (Acts 13:27-29; 17:3).

This scriptural plan of God was very important for Luke's audience. It explained not only the meaning of Christ's suffering and death but also the value of that experience for them. Only a powerful divine plan could give them hope and meaning when they were faced by trial, persecution, and possibly death. For that reason Luke is careful to apply it to Paul, who would be a special model for his audience. Paul returned to Lystra, Iconium, and Antioch, appointing successors and reminding them that "through many tribulations we must enter the kingdom of God" (Acts 14:22). This was a direct parallel to Jesus, who announced that he had entered the kingdom and glory by the same path. The risen Jesus said to the disciples on the way to Emmaus: "Was it not necessary that the Christ should suffer these things and enter into his glory?" (Luke 24:26).

The Acts of the Apostles dwells at length on the sufferings, the persecution, and even the death faced by the audience's past leaders, who are a model for them in similar experiences. For example, Stephen, one of the "Seven" (Acts 6:1-6), was seized and stoned to death by Jewish leaders. Just before his death he saw the heavens opened and the Son of man standing to receive him. His dying prayer was for the forgiveness of others, "Lord, do not hold this sin against them" (Acts 7:60). As a result of this prayer, Paul ceased persecuting the Church and became its greatest apostle. Luke patterned Stephen's death on that of Jesus. Stephen was the first martyr, an example for those of the audience who follow him. As we pointed out in our discussion of the Gospel of Mark, their suffering and even death could be the best way to win over others.

Luke's "Omission" of the Anointing at Bethany and Its Significance

We have placed the word "omission" in quotation marks because Luke does not place the anointing at Bethany before the passion account, as Matthew and Mark do. However, he has transformed the story and used it in another place for important reasons—reasons very closely connected to the meaning of Jesus' death as he has presented it. We have seen how important the anointing was for both Matthew and Mark, since they connected it to the essential meaning of Jesus' death. Luke, though, cannot put the anointing before Jesus' passion because it implies some kind of foreknowledge by others (at least in Mark) of what is going to happen—Jesus' death and burial. For Luke this whole matter is hidden in the divine plan. It is a secret known only to Jesus and revealed to others after his resurrection. Mary Magdalene and the others were the first ones to remember his word and bring it to others.

Luke does know about the anointing at Bethany and transforms it in order to bring it in line with the central message of Jesus' death as he understands it. He places it in his account of the penitent woman (Luke 7:36-50). To discover its significance, we must first continue and complete the theme of the Christ who "could not save himself." Luke wants to show that Jesus could not do so in obedience to the divine plan: that he might be able to save all in a great, surprising reversal. Luke brings this out in the very last episode before Jesus' death:

> One of the criminals who were hanged railed at him, saying, "Are you not the Christ? Save yourself and us!" But the other rebuked him, saying, "Do you not fear God, since you are under the same sentence of condemnation? And we indeed justly; for we are receiving the due reward of our deeds; but this man has done nothing wrong." And he said, "Jesus, remember me when you come in your kingly power." And he said to him, "Truly, I say to you, today you will be with me in Paradise" (Luke 23:39-43).

Luke's drama reaches its climax when one of those crucified with Jesus repents and pleads, "Jesus, remember me when you come in your kingly power" (Luke 23:42). Luke highlights this request because this man is the first to call upon the name of Jesus in view of his death and be saved. In the Acts of the Apostles, Luke will demonstrate that the ultimate purpose of Jesus' death, resurrection, and gift of the Spirit is that "whoever calls on the name of the Lord shall be saved" (Acts 2:21). To bring out maximum impact on the audience, Luke calls this crucified man a "criminal" (*kakourgos*) three times (Luke 23:32, 33, 39). Mark and Matthew called the two other crucified men *lēstai*, "robbers" or "revolutionaries" (Mark 15:27; Matt 27:38). Luke makes the change to "criminal" to show his audience that anyone, even a person in the most desperate situation or after a long life of crime, could identify with the criminal and thus have hope. Jesus' immediate promise of forgiveness and happiness in Paradise *today* (Luke 23:43) simply cannot be surpassed as an act of compassion and mercy.

This scene reinforces the majestic image of Jesus that Luke has been presenting. Jesus appears to be in complete mastery of the situation. He knows when he is going to die and confidently prays the words of Psalm 31, "Into your hands I commit my spirit," before breathing his last (Luke 23:46). As Lord and Judge, he dispenses the rewards of the kingdom to the repentant criminal.[37] As Judge, even while carrying his cross to execution, he speaks with the women of Jerusalem and foretells the consequences of the actions of those who are leading him to death (Luke 23:28-31).

This stress on Jesus' name and person on the cross prepares the way for the Acts of the Apostles, where calling on Jesus' name is the distinguishing mark of a believer. This was built on the conviction that Jesus became universal Lord and Christ through his death and resurrection. Peter had stated this on Pentecost: "Let all the house of Israel know assuredly that God has made both Lord and Christ, this Jesus whom you crucified" (Acts 2:36). Anyone can call upon his name with perfect confidence and fulfill the prophecy of Joel: "All who call upon the name of the Lord shall be delivered" (Joel 2:32).

The title LORD applied to Jesus had tremendous implications in view of its biblical background. LORD was the name pronounced as a substitute for God's mysterious, unutterable name, YAHWEH, revealed to Moses from the burning bush (Exod 3:14). Because of Jesus' enthronement in the kingdom at his death, Christians believed that this powerful name was transferred to him. This name had an awesome history in the Bible. For example, in the burning bush it meant inexhaustible energy; in the miraculous exodus from Egypt, it signified invincible leadership and power: "And the LORD went before them by day in a pillar of cloud to lead them along the way, and by night in a pillar of fire to give them light" (Exod 13:21). On Mount Sinai the LORD gave the people a covenant in a thunderous voice accompanied by earthquakes from a smoking, fiery mountain (Exod 19:18-20).

The Acts of the Apostles is filled with examples of the use and power of the great NAME. The first experience of this name for believers was at their baptism, as indicated in Peter's appeal: "Repent, and be baptized every one of you in the *name* of Jesus Christ for the forgiveness of your sins; and you shall receive the gift of the Holy Spirit" (Acts 2:38). At baptism a person called on Jesus' name for the first time, as Paul and others did at their conversion and baptism (Acts 8:16; 10:48; 19:8). Baptism meant a deep interrelationship with Christ as he entrusted his name (person) to the disciple. The same was true of God's revelation of his name to Moses. This gave him the privilege of calling on that name with complete confidence and with power.

The importance of the NAME was so great that Christians were distinguished as "those who call on his name" (see Acts 9:14). This name empowered a believer to act in the person of Jesus and with his power. Thus Peter raised up a lame man by the Temple gate with the name of Jesus (Acts 3:1-10). Peter and John taught in Jesus' name with power and authority (Acts 4:18). To suffer for Jesus was to suffer for his name (Acts 9:16). It was even a privilege and a joy to do so (Acts 5:41). Paul declared that he was even willing to die for the name of the Lord Jesus (Acts 21:13).

Returning to the crucifixion, we see how important it was for Luke to stress that the Christ who could not save himself could indeed save others, even those in the most desperate circumstances. This was because Jesus entered into the kingdom at his death and received full power to save others. Luke distinguishes two groups present at the crucifixion—those who understand what is happening and repent, and those who are enemies of Christ. Immediately after the centurion's acclamation, Luke writes, "All the multitudes who assembled to see the sight, when they saw what had taken place, returned home beating their breasts" (Luke 23:48). Immediately after this, Luke mentions the women and Jesus' acquaintances, who would certainly have been among those who personally appreciated Jesus' death. Right from the beginning of his Gospel, Luke has emphasized this attitude of a humble sinner in regard to Christ. When Peter is called, he responds to Jesus' miraculous draught of fish with the words, "Depart from me, for I am a sinful man, O Lord" (Luke 5:8). The same holds true in regard to Mary Magdalene. Luke describes her as one "from whom seven demons had gone out" (Luke 8:2). This hints at the type of conversion that took place in her.

With all this in mind, we can see why Luke has transferred and transformed the anointing by the woman at Bethany. First of all, we should note the common details in the narrative of the penitent woman in Luke 7:36-50 and the anointing at Bethany in Mark's Gospel (Mark 14:3-9) which suggest that they were originally the same story: a certain Simon is the host in both stories; the alabaster jar of ointment appears in both; the anointing of Jesus occurs in both stories, but in Luke the ointment is poured on Jesus' feet, not on his head, perhaps to avoid the hint of a messianic ointment. In both accounts Jesus appears as a prophet who knows the thoughts of his host and others.

Luke describes this anointing in great detail to make it correspond to his central teaching on Jesus' death, namely, that those who call upon his name will be saved. On the part of the woman, this is nonverbal. She comes to Jesus and shows him hospitality—a willingness to receive him into "her house"—by washing his feet with her tears and then anointing them with oil. All this is accompanied by the kisses that should welcome a guest. The letting down of her hair was a symbol of her love and devotion. The meaning of her action is brought out by Jesus' words to the Pharisee host, "I entered your house, you gave me no water for my feet, but she has wet my feet with her tears and wiped them with her hair. You gave me no kiss, but from the time I came in she has not ceased to kiss my feet. You did not anoint my head with oil, but she has anointed my feet with ointment" (Luke 7:44-46).

These words show that the woman has truly received Jesus by extending the traditional signs of hospitality in an extraordinary way. This contrasts with the cold omission of these signs by the Pharisee, who did not feel the need of repentance and forgiveness. Thus Jesus can say to the woman, "Therefore I tell you, her sins, which are many, are forgiven, for she loved much; but the one who is forgiven little, loves little. And he said to her, 'Your sins are forgiven' " (Luke 7:47).

Luke notes that those at table said among themselves, "Who is this, who even forgives sins?" (Luke 7:49), indicating that there is some question of blasphemy in regard to a matter that is the province only of God. This is similar to the story of the paralytic, where a similar objection is made (Luke 5:17-26). Finally, the story closes with Jesus' statement to the woman: "Your faith has saved you; go in peace" (Luke 7:50). Thus Jesus' saving and forgiving action is similar to his saving of the "good thief" on the cross. The woman calls on Jesus through her nonverbal, symbolic action of loving hospitality and receives forgiveness.

Luke's introduction to the story brings out its exemplary nature. Jesus has been contrasted with the Baptist as being "a glutton and a drunkard, a friend of tax collectors and sinners" (Luke 7:34). The story shows that Jesus indeed is such a friend, but in a much deeper sense. It has been suggested that the woman had already been forgiven as a convert of the Baptist.[38] However, details of the story point to an encounter with Jesus, leading to his last statement assuring the woman of forgiveness and salvation.

We can see why Luke has given such attention to this story and transformed the original narrative of the anointing at Bethany. He wishes to highlight the woman's anointing as a special example of the saving effect of the cross, and thus place it in direct correspondence with the story of Jesus' death. Right after the anointing we have the first mention of the women who accompanied Jesus on his journey, especially Mary Magdalene. Luke may have done this to bring out that the woman who anointed Jesus became his follower. The conversion of this woman, who had been a "sinner" (Luke 7:37), is like that of Mary Magdalene, "from whom seven demons had gone out" (Luke 8:2). It is not certain whether Luke identifies Mary Magdalene with the penitent woman; if so, it would further enhance Mary Magdalene as a hero of the Gospel in view of the connection of the story with the saving events of the cross.

Mary, the Mother of Jesus and the Mother of Believers

Strictly speaking, Mary cannot be called a Gospel hero, since she is not a disciple who follows Jesus all the way to the cross. However, she is closely connected to Mary Magdalene's essential role as one of those who first remembered Jesus' "impossible" word about his coming suffering and death according to the divine plan. Luke is anxious to portray Mary as one who listens to God's word through the message of an angel and believes, no matter how impossible it might seem. In this way she is a model for those who would later accept the most difficult scriptures about Jesus' suffering and death as God's plan for salvation.

Luke brings out Mary's role model by paralleling the beginning and ending of his Gospel. It begins with the promise of new life for the world, first by the birth of the Baptist, and then by the birth of Jesus: "And she gave birth to her first-born son and wrapped him in swaddling cloths, and laid him in a manger, because there was no place for them in the inn" (Luke 2:7). Mary, like Mary Magdalene and the others at the tomb, is a supreme witness of the utter humanity of the child, in contrast to the errors of docetism. At Jesus' birth she wrapped the child in swaddling clothes, like every other human child. The account of his birth bears similarities to that of his death: the women watched as Joseph of Arimathea *"wrapped* it [Jesus' body] in a linen shroud, and *laid* him in a rock-hewn tomb" (Luke 24:53).

Like the account of Jesus' birth, the resurrection accounts focus on the gift of new life. The angels at the tomb tell the women, "Why do you seek the living among the dead? He is not here" (Luke 24:5). Luke is the only one who calls Jesus the "living" one. He does this to explain the resurrection of Jesus as a new birth and source of new life for the world. This same theme of new life is repeated in the Acts of the Apostles.

Peter said to the Temple crowd, "You . . . asked for a mur-
derer to be granted to you, and killed the Author of life, whom
God raised from the dead" (Acts 3:14). Just as Mary brought
the child Jesus into the world, so the women at the tomb seem
to be pictured as mediators of life, bringing the first announcement of new life in the risen Jesus to others.

A second important part that Mary plays in Luke's Gospel
is in regard to the followers of John the Baptist, who did not
all turn to Jesus after the death of John. Many of them simply
continued as the Baptist's disciples. Christians came into con-
tact with them in various parts of the Greek world. For example, Luke tells us that Aquila and Priscilla found Apollos,
a noted preacher and disciple of the Baptist, at Ephesus (Acts
18:24-28). Paul came upon a group of the Baptist's disciples
in the same city. He explained to them that John's baptism was
to prepare for Jesus' baptism of the Holy Spirit and then converted them (Acts 19:1-7).

The question of the priority of the Baptist over Jesus was
a very vital one for these followers of the Baptist. The first chapters of Luke contain remarkable stories about the birth of John.
Therefore Luke was anxious to compare the origins of Jesus
with those of the Baptist and to show that Jesus' origins were
far superior. As a result, we find that Mary's role in these chapters takes on additional importance.

In what follows we will sketch Luke's portrait of Mary as
a model for believers in view of the above concerns.[39] First of
all, Luke narrates the story of the miraculous birth of the Baptist. The scriptural model for John's birth to his aged parents,
Zechariah and Elizabeth, was the birth of Isaac to Abraham
and Sarah in their old age (Gen 21:1-7). That birth was such
a surprise that both Abraham and Sarah laughed when God
announced it to them (Gen 17:17; 18:12-15). When the child
was born, Sarah exclaimed, "God has made laughter for me;
every one who hears will laugh over me" (Gen 21:6). Most
appropriately, then, the boy was called Isaac, meaning
"laughter."

Abraham had the supreme title of father of the Jewish people, while Sarah was regarded as the great mother. Isaiah wrote, "Look to Abraham your father and to Sarah who bore you" (Isa 51:2). So in view of the impressive tradition of the miraculous birth of John the Baptist, modeled on that of Isaac, it was essential for Luke to present Jesus' birth as even greater. Hence he will describe how the faith of Jesus' mother surpassed even that of Abraham, and how her motherhood was even greater than that of Sarah. Likewise, Luke will show how Mary surpassed Zechariah and Elizabeth, the parents of the Baptist, in faith and attitude.

When the angel announced the birth of the Baptist to Zechariah the priest, he was so shocked that he could not believe it. He replied to the angel, "How shall I know this? For I am an old man, and my wife is advanced in years" (Luke 1:18). As a punishment for his disbelief and as a sign, the angel Gabriel told him that he would be literally "dumbfounded," unable to speak until God's word was fulfilled.

In contrast, Luke relates the story of the same angel's annunciation of Jesus' birth to Mary and describes her reaction:

> In the sixth month the angel Gabriel was sent from God to a city of Galilee named Nazareth, to a virgin betrothed to a man whose name was Joseph, of the house of David; and the virgin's name was Mary. And he came to her and said, "Hail, O favored one, the Lord is with you!" But she was greatly troubled at the saying, and considered in her mind what sort of greeting this might be. And the angel said to her, "Do not be afraid, Mary, for you have found favor with God. And behold you will conceive in your womb and bear a son, and you shall call his name Jesus. He will be great, and will be called the Son of the Most High" (Luke 1:26-32).

The same angel Gabriel who appeared to Zechariah comes also to Mary. Abraham and Sarah had both received new names from God in view of their new role in the divine plan (Gen 17:5, 15). Likewise, God, through the angel, also gives Mary a new name, *kecharitōmenē*, meaning "favored one," from the Greek root *charis*, meaning "grace" or "favor." In accord with biblical custom, the new name is then explained: "You have found favor with God." The word *kecharitōmenē* also has the meaning of "beautiful one."[40] Luke may have in mind a comparison with Sarah, whose great beauty receives special mention in the Bible (Gen 12:10-15) and became legendary in Jewish tradition.[41] However, Luke brings in a subtle contrast: Mary's beauty or favor is from within; it is "with God."

While Sarah's conceiving in old age was extraordinary, that of Mary was absolutely impossible. She is called a virgin twice in the story (Luke 1:27) and must ask the angel, "How can this be since [literally] I do not know man?" (Luke 1:34). The angel replies to her, "The Holy Spirit will come upon you, and the power of the Most High will overshadow you; therefore the child to be born will be called holy, the Son of God." Thus the child will not only be virginally conceived by the Holy Spirit but will also be the long-awaited Messiah, Son of God, and therefore his birth will be the most important birth in human history.

The angel then tells Mary that her cousin Elizabeth has also conceived in her old age and adds, "With God nothing will be impossible." Mary then assents to the angel with faith and humility: "Behold, I am the handmaid of the Lord; let it be to me according to your word" (Luke 1:38). Thus Mary's faith and the birth of her child are more extraordinary than even the faith of Abraham and Sarah and the birth of Isaac.

Next, Mary's visit to her cousin Elizabeth places additional emphasis on Mary as a model for believers. When Mary entered Elizabeth's house and greeted her, Elizabeth felt the child in her womb leap and interpreted this as an unusual sign. Luke notes that Elizabeth was filled with the Holy Spirit and cried out with a loud voice (Luke 1:42). This means that what she said was directly inspired by God and of great importance to the Gospel audience. Elizabeth said: "Blessed are you among women, and blessed is the fruit of your womb! And why is this granted to me, that the mother of my Lord should come to me? For behold, when the voice of your greeting came to my ears, the babe in my womb leaped for joy. And blessed is she who believed that there would be a fulfillment of what was spoken to her from the Lord'' (Luke 1:42-45).

We note especially the words ''Blessed is she who believed,'' inspired by the Holy Spirit and directed toward Mary. Luke proposes her as a model for believers, since she accepted the angel's word despite its human impossibility. These words of Elizabeth are echoed by Mary in her responding song of praise, the *Magnificat*. She declares, ''All generations will call me blessed; for he who is mighty has done great things for me'' (Luke 1:48). Since Luke wrote this about two generations afterward, he describes a view of Mary held long after her death. The Holy Spirit in the community continues to say of her, ''Blessed is she who believed.''

In the title of this section, we named Mary as ''*mother* of believers.'' What basis is there in Luke that he and his community thought of her as a mother? First of all, we have noted the parallels between the Gospel of Luke and the Acts of the Apostles. Luke begins with the Holy Spirit overshadowing Mary so that she becomes the mother of the Christ. The Acts of the Apostles also begins with the descent of the Holy Spirit on the first believers.

As the mother of Jesus made possible the birth of Jesus through the Holy Spirit, so also she takes part in the parallel birth of the Church through the Holy Spirit. Luke gives her prominence among those who were present: the apostles, ''together with the women and Mary the mother of Jesus, and with his brethren'' (Acts 1:13-14). Since Jesus' disciples were a new family in which the titles ''brother'' and ''sister'' were given to those of the same age, while the titles ''mother'' and ''father'' were given to those who were older (Luke 8:19-21) the title ''mother'' would certainly be appropriate for one so preeminent as Mary, the mother of Jesus.

A second basis for calling Mary the ''mother of believers'' emerges by way of comparison with Abraham and Sarah.

Abraham was the father of the Jews, and Sarah the great mother. Since Mary was superior to each of them, she could be considered a mother of believers also. Such a way of thinking is supported in the New Testament. Abraham is called "the father of all who believe" (Rom 4:11). Sarah's faith is also praised in Hebrews 11:11. Christians are called "her [Sarah's] children" if they imitate her example (1 Pet 3:6). If these descriptions were applied to Abraham and Sarah, they would be all the more applicable to Mary, the mother of Jesus and of believers.

There is a final reason why the title "mother" would be very important for Luke's community. The Acts of the Apostles gives special attention to Paul's apostolate at Ephesus, the capital of the Roman province of Asia and one of the largest cities of the empire. It was also the center of the cult of Artemis, the great mother-goddess. Her ancient temple at Ephesus was one of the seven wonders of the ancient world, attracting pilgrims not only from Roman Asia but from many parts of Europe as well. The great center of attraction was the renowned image of Artemis that the town clerk described in this manner: "Men of Ephesus, what man is there who does not know that the city of the Ephesians is temple keeper of the great Artemis, and of the sacred stone that fell from the sky?" (Acts 19:35).

While the translation "sacred stone" is not certain, it certainly refers to the famous image of Artemis. Archaeologists have found many statuettes of her, probably replicas of a larger one. They are distinguished by fertility symbols featuring dozens of breasts or wheat clusters. It is no wonder that Luke gives so much attention to the riot of silversmiths at Ephesus. These people were profoundly disturbed by the growing Christian community and the sharp decline in demand for Artemis' images. A certain Demetrius gathered together his fellow silversmiths and said to them, "Men, you know that from this business we have our wealth. And you see and hear that not only at Ephesus but almost throughout all Asia this Paul has persuaded and turned away a considerable company of people, saying that gods made with hands are not gods'' (Acts 19:25-26). Luke spends considerable time with this story, showing how important it was for him and his audience.

Demetrius continued, ''There is danger not only that this trade of ours may come into disrepute but also that the temple of the great goddess Artemis may count for nothing, and that she may even be deposed from her magnificence, she whom all Asia and the world worship'' (Acts 19:27). The silversmiths then went in procession around the city, chanting, ''Great is Artemis of the Ephesians!'' Then they gathered a large crowd in the theater, where for two hours they kept up a thunderous ovation with the same chant (Acts 19:34).

It would be most interesting to know how this powerful former worship of Artemis affected new converts. The loss of the deeply loved and revered mother-goddess must have been greatly felt. This loss was made especially acute because Christianity was more male-oriented around Jesus as Savior. It is indeed quite plausible that Luke's presentation of Mary as mother of believers would have been influenced by the need of converts who were accustomed to a deep feminine element in their lives and worship.

CHAPTER FOUR

THE GOSPEL OF JOHN

"Standing by the cross of Jesus were his mother,
and . . . Mary Magdalene" (John 19:25)

Strictly speaking, the Gospel of John can have no women or men as counterparts of Jesus because it centers about the journey of the Logos, the Word of God, into this world and its return to God. The Gospel announces this in its opening line: "In the beginning was the Word, and the Word was with God, and the Word was God . . . all things were made through him" (1:1). This Word incarnates itself in Jesus: "And the Word became flesh and dwelt among us" (1:14). At the end of Jesus' life the incarnate Word returns to God. At the Last Supper, the evangelist notes, "Jesus, knowing that the Father had given all things into his hands, and that he had come from God and was going to God, rose from supper . . ." (13:3-4). In his last testament in chapters 14 to 16, Jesus announces that he is returning to his "Father's house" (14:2) and describes how his disciples can follow him there.

We notice immediately how different John's Gospel is from those of Matthew, Mark, and Luke. In those Gospels we had a journey of Jesus from Galilee to Jerusalem, where he faced the cross and death. He invited others to follow him along the same journey. Jesus is the hero of those Gospels, and thus we can have a counterpart in an ideal disciple. In John's Gospel we still have the journey of Jesus to the cross and death; however, it is more like the external part of the journey, while the real, internal part is the journey of the Logos into this world and then its return to God. This external journey, through the use of signs, is a way to enter into a relationship with the eternal Word acting in Jesus.

At the end of this journey, Jesus does not leave his disciples alone. He promises them an inner successor, the Paraclete, who will always remain with them and lead them back to the Father, where they can rejoin Jesus. In his last testament and farewell discourse, Jesus tells his disciples: "These things I have spoken to you, while I am still with you. But the Counselor (*paraklētos*), the Holy Spirit, whom the Father will send in my name, will teach you all things, and bring to your remembrance all that I have said to you" (14:25-26).

This Holy Spirit will not only succeed Jesus but will help his disciples experience his presence and understand his teaching in a new generation. In this way it will serve as a "double" for Jesus. However, this Spirit will embody itself in the community, and especially in certain "outer successors" of Jesus. Among these, the Gospel of John singles out a "disciple whom Jesus loved," who reclines on Jesus' bosom at the Last Supper. Even Peter, the head of the Twelve, asks this disciple to intercede with Jesus to find out who will betray Jesus (13:23-26). This disciple is the special source behind the Gospel of John and its special understanding of Jesus' message. In order to present his credentials, the Gospel author describes him at the foot of the cross, where Jesus confirms his special relationship to him: "Standing by the cross of Jesus were his mother, and his mother's sister, Mary the wife of Clopas, and Mary Magdalene. When Jesus saw his mother, and the disciple whom he loved standing near, he said to his mother, 'Woman, behold, your son!' Then he said to the disciple, 'Behold, your mother!' And from that hour the disciple took her to his own home" (19:25-27).

We note that the Gospel of John presents the Beloved Disciple, the mother of Jesus, and Mary Magdalene as the witnesses of Jesus' death, the great "hour" so often mentioned in the Gospel. Here the interconnection between Jesus' mother and the Beloved Disciple will be our first concern. The author must present his source and teacher, the Beloved Disciple, with the best possible credentials. He must be someone very closely related to Jesus so that he can be considered an authoritative successor like Peter, James, the brother of the Lord, and others.

In the above passage Jesus tells his mother, "Woman, behold, your son!" (in reference to the Beloved Disciple), and then he tells the disciple, "Behold, your mother!" (19:26-27). These words are not simply a last command of Jesus that a favorite disciple take care of his mother. They must be understood in view of the special place that the Beloved Disciple has for the Gospel audience. He is their founder, and a close relationship with Jesus' mother would guarantee that he has the right to be a successor to Jesus and interpreter of the meaning of his death. The words "Behold, your mother" are a revelatory formula introducing a new role as mother that Mary will exercise in regard to the Beloved Disciple and his community.[42] These words establish him as a "brother" or special relative of Jesus—so much so that Jesus' mother will adopt him into her own family.

In this regard Raymond Brown has written, "By stressing not only that his mother has become the mother of the beloved disciple, but also that the disciple has become her son, the Johannine Jesus is logically claiming the disciple as his true brother."[43] A last word of Jesus confirming a relationship between this disciple and his mother would be most significant. It would establish him as a "brother of the Lord," with authority like that of James, Jesus' blood relative, or other disciples of Jesus, even Peter.

Mary is important not only in this episode but within the literary structure and meaning of the whole Gospel. This will become evident when we closely examine this structure. The Fourth Gospel has a series of signs, beginning with the story of the wedding feast at Cana, which ends with the statement, "This, the first of his signs, Jesus did at Cana in Galilee, and manifested his glory; and his disciples believed in him" (2:11).

The usual assumption has been that the first twelve chapters of John's Gospel contain the principal signs. Many Bibles even divide the Gospel into two parts, calling these first twelve chapters "The Book of Signs."

These signs have usually been considered to be seven in number: (1) the wedding at Cana (2:1-12); (2) the raising of the dying son of the royal official (4:46-54); (3) the healing of the paralytic on the sabbath (5:1-18); (4) the multiplication of loaves (6:1-15); (5) Jesus' walking on water (6:16-22); (6) the healing of the blind man on the sabbath (9:1-41); and (7) the restoration of Lazarus to life (11:1-54). However, M. Girard has provided us with important reasons to conclude that the evangelist did not intend the above arrangement.[44] We will summarize his arguments, for they will be important in discovering the central place of Jesus' mother in this Gospel. First of all, Girard accepts Raymond Brown's definition of a sign as a prodigious deed with strong symbolism illustrating Jesus' salvific message.[45] According to this definition, the fifth sign, Jesus' walking on water, simply does not fit. Instead, it looks like a part of the total message of the discourse at the multiplication of loaves, perhaps suggesting a Passover context. The actual use of the word "sign" is another indication. This word is not used in reference to Jesus' walking on the water, in contrast to all the others: 1:11; 4:54; 6:2 (in reference to the previous healing at Bethesda); 9:16 and 12:18 (about the raising of Lazarus).

That would leave us with only six signs. What is the seventh sign, if there is one? The evangelist does appear to be counting them; he calls Cana the first (2:11) and the raising of the official's son the second (4:54). It would appear strange for him to have only six signs, like the incomplete six water jars at Cana! In looking for a seventh sign, there is really no strong reason to conclude the signs with the so-called "end of the signs book" in 12:37-50, where the author writes, "Though he had done so many signs before them, yet they did not believe in him" (12:37). This may only mean that the previous six signs are incomplete and insufficient. This hypothesis is strengthened by the author's conclusion (if chapter 21 is an appendix) after Jesus' death that "these [signs] are written that you may believe that Jesus is the Christ, the Son of God . . ." (20:31).

Girard points out that the real seventh sign is Jesus' death and the extraordinary flow of blood and water from his side. The Beloved Disciple, who witnessed it along with the mother of Jesus and Mary Magdalene, considered it so unusual that he made a special claim to be an eyewitness so that others might believe as well (19:35). As a result, the first six signs are meant to be incomplete and point to the seventh at Jesus' "hour," when he will be lifted up and draw the world to himself (12:32-33). The specific word "sign" is not used here, perhaps because the author wanted to save it for his final conclusion in 20:31 (quoted above).

However, I would suggest that the Passover connections to Jesus' death are so strong that the audience would surely realize that the meaning of the Passover ritual came to a climax with the "sign of the blood" of the Passover lamb: "The blood shall be a sign for you, upon the houses where you are: and when I see the blood, I will pass over you, and no plague shall fall upon you to destroy you, when I smite the land of Egypt" (Exod 12:13). The Beloved Disciple actually *saw* the sign of the blood as he stood beneath the cross (19:35) and witnessed the blood and water flowing from the side of Jesus. Such a flow of blood was considered a necessary part of any sacrifice. This has been illustrated by the studies of J. M. Ford.[46]

With this as a seventh sign, Girard has discovered the following chiastic structure of the seven signs:

1) The wedding feast at Cana (2:1-12)
2) The raising of the dying son of the official (4:46-54)
3) The healing on the sabbath at Bethesda (5:1-16)
4) The loaves' multiplication and the bread of life (6:1-71)
5) The healing of the blind man on the sabbath (9:1-41)

6) The raising of Lazarus (11:1-41)

7) The hour of Jesus and the issue of blood and water (19:25-38)

We immediately notice the striking parallels: signs 3 and 5 are both healings on the sabbath; 2 and 6 contain the same theme of death to life because of Jesus' word; 1 and 7 complement one another as beginning and end, with Jesus' mother present at both. She witnessed Jesus' obedience to his Father on the cross, culminating with the drink of bitter wine according to the Scriptures. As a parallel, at Cana Mary asked for obedience to Jesus' word, ending in the chief steward's taking the "cup" of good wine.

The essential place of Mary is strengthened by this literary structure of the seven signs: Jesus' mother is present at the first sign at Cana (2:1-11) and at the seventh sign at the cross (19:25-37). She is also named in the central sign of the multiplication of loaves (6:42, in most manuscripts). The best place to begin studying her key role is in the last and seventh sign at the cross.

The Mother of Jesus in the Seventh Sign

We note that Mary is present in the most important first and last signs. Both open up with her presence. In the episode of the wedding at Cana, the word "mother" is used four times and "woman" once (2:1-11); in the seventh sign "mother" is found four times and "woman" once (19:25, 26, 27). Thus the writer appears to be deliberately making a close connection between the two episodes.

The seventh sign begins with the statement that Jesus' mother stood by the cross along with Mary Magdalene and the Beloved Disciple. Thus Mary is an essential witness of these central events. The question of historicity (since she is not present there in the other Gospels) need not detain us; the Fourth Gospel uses the words "see" and "know" in deeper senses. For example, even the blind can "see" if they understand

Jesus' words (9:39). By the time John's Gospel was written, Mary had almost certainly been dead for many years, yet the author wrote as if the events described had a present meaning for his audience: "he tells the truth—that you also may believe" (19:35). Since the whole Gospel of John has the element of timeless drama, the events at the cross may have this atmosphere also. In this Gospel the risen Jesus still bears the marks of the cross and the spear (20:20, 24). In our study we are taking the Gospel "as is" for our primary source, since this is the way the audience heard it.

During the seventh sign the Beloved Disciple makes a key eyewitness testimony after he observes water and blood coming out of Jesus' side after the lance thrust: "He who saw it has borne witness—his testimony is true, and he knows that he tells the truth—that you also may believe" (19:35). He makes this solemn statement because he perceived the special sign-meaning in the unusual flow of watery blood from Jesus' side. As suggested above, he may have seen it as the "sign of the blood" of the Passover lamb that God had promised to the people (Exod 12:13). This Passover emphasis goes along with the writer's announcement of the fulfillment of the Scriptures in regard to the Passover lamb ritual: "Not a bone of him shall be broken" (19:36).

The evangelist wishes to stress that the meaning of Jesus' death is found in the fulfillment of the Passover ritual. By his death Jesus became the true Passover sacrificial lamb whose flesh is to be consumed (mentioned three times in 6:52-58) and whose sprinkled blood brings salvation. Such a teaching requires an unmistakable stamp of credibility. That is why Jesus' last testament on the cross establishes the Beloved Disciple as his successor by having his own mother continue the relationship with him as mother and son.

Jesus' mother functions as a joint witness along with the Beloved Disciple of these key events in Jesus' life and their meaning. Together they witness the seventh sign of the unusual flow of watery blood from Jesus' side. In addition, Mary acts as a mother by witnessing the utter reality of Jesus' death. A mother's indelible memory of her child is a popular perception found in Isaiah 49:15, where God says, "Can a woman forget her sucking child, that she should have no compassion on the son of her womb?" This memory is especially true regarding a child's death. Mary has a special function as mother to the community of the Beloved Disciple. As one who remembers, she is a carrier of tradition, which is a supreme function of a mother. Her association with Jesus in any teaching about him would be a continual reminder of his death and its meaning as explained in the Fourth Gospel.

In a chiastic pattern, such as the seven signs, the beginning and the end point to the middle, which in this case is the fourth sign of the loaves. Therefore we would expect the seventh and first signs to complete the meaning of the fourth sign of the loaves and answer questions about it. Answers to questions about Jesus' divinity as well as his humanity and death would be very important for understanding the central sign of the loaves. The joint witness of Jesus' mother and the Beloved Disciple would be necessary to answer questions about the flesh-and-blood reality of Jesus in the sign of the loaves. This is such a difficult teaching that many disciples part from Jesus because of his statements about eating his flesh and drinking his blood (6:52-66).

The Fourth Gospel, therefore, presents Jesus' mother along with the Beloved Disciple as essential witnesses as to *how* Jesus died. The first key point is that Jesus died on the cross in perfect obedience to his Father. To bring this out, the author stresses Jesus' obedience to God's plan as found in the Scriptures (19:24, 28, 30). Special focus is placed on Psalm 69:21, "For my thirst they gave me vinegar to drink." The evangelist has Jesus very deliberately saying, "I thirst," and then taking the bitter drink (19:28-30). Jesus takes it in obedience to the scriptures of Psalm 69, which were considered God's plan.

Later we will notice in the first sign that Mary will direct the "waiters" to do everything that Jesus says (2:5). The "good wine" will be made possible through obedience to Jesus' word, just as he has been obedient to the Father by accepting the "bitter wine" on the cross. Jesus' last words after taking the wine are, "It is finished" (19:30). These words bring out that he has been obedient to the moment of his death by his last action of drinking the "final cup" of bitter wine. Thus he has finished or completed his own life as well as God's plan in the Scriptures. In this way Jesus' previous words at his arrest are literally fulfilled: "Shall I not drink the cup which the Father has given me?" (18:11).

In addition to witnessing this obedience, Jesus' mother is a key witness of other events in Jesus' death that point to a divine element within him. The Gospel describes a majestic Jesus supremely in control on the cross. He knows exactly when he is going to die (19:28); then he says that it is all finished (19:30); and finally he seems to deliberately bow his head and expire. This was predicted earlier when Jesus said that no one takes away his life from him; he dies by his own choice. He has the power to lay down his life and to take it up again, in accord with the Father's command (10:18). This sign indicates something suprahuman in Jesus' death. It is a real death, yet no human being has the power to determine when life will come and when it will go. In the Bible, only God has this power.

This divine choice is carefully presented in the Gospel. The author describes how the Word came into the world to be born in the flesh by his own choice; now he dies in the same way. All this, in parallel to Jesus' death, points to an inner divine element in Jesus, and his mother is a witness of this. With the interconnection of the seventh sign and that of the loaves, we find an answer to the question of the Jews, "How does he now say, 'I have come down from heaven'?" (6:42). It is noteworthy that immediately after this, in the next verse, Jesus' mother is mentioned (in some Greek manuscripts). The emphasis on Jesus' divinity, as well as the voluntary nature of Jesus' death, would be essential to show that he is the real priest who offers himself, the Paschal Lamb, to the Father. The Jewish priests and Pilate are only indirect instruments used by God.

Finally, Jesus' mother is the supreme witness of *how Jesus died*, especially regarding his motivation. Jesus' motive was obedience to the Father, but it was not mechanical conformity. It was a submission prompted by love for his disciples and for the world. God's will is to save the whole human family through the death of his Son: "God so loved the world that he gave his only Son" (3:16). As for Jesus himself, the writer notes before his account of the Last Supper that Jesus loved his disciples "to the end" (13:1). The expression "to the end" may mean to the fullest extent, but it would likely include the completion on the cross when Jesus said it was finished (19:30).

This motivation of love comes out clearly in the raising of Lazarus. When Jesus decided to go into Judea to help Lazarus, his disciples were alarmed because they knew that the Master's life was in danger there (11:8). However, Jesus resolved to go, knowing that this would lead to his own death. Thus the writer brings out symbolically (since Lazarus' resurrection symbolizes that of believers) that Jesus died out of love in order to make others live. For this reason the Gospel notes that Jesus loved Lazarus, Martha, and Mary (11:5). The mother of Jesus at the cross, along with the Beloved Disciple, is a special witness of this motivating love. They saw that Jesus loved his disciples "to the end."

To sum up, Jesus' mother can guarantee the authenticity of the Beloved Disciple's teaching on the reality and meaning of Jesus' death. She can do this because of Jesus' last testament leaving the Beloved Disciple to take his place as her son. This establishes the Beloved Disciple as a successor of Jesus. Mary at the cross is also an essential witness of the reality of Jesus' humanity as well as his divinity. She confirms the meaning of Jesus' death as the new Passover Lamb. This explains how Jesus can command in the sign of the loaves that his flesh be eaten and his blood consumed (6:52-55). The believer's participation in this will now be explained in the first sign at Cana.

Jesus' Mother in the First Sign at Cana of Galilee (2:1-12)

The chiastic arrangement of the seven signs leads us to expect a close relationship between the first, fourth, and seventh signs. The first is included in the last, and the last completes the first; both illustrate the fourth and central sign of the multiplication of loaves. In the texts we find elements common to all three, especially the first and last: Jesus' mother, the "hour" on the cross (2:4), the thirst or lack of wine, the obedience motif, the wine/blood/water.

As the Cana story opens, Jesus' mother is present at a wedding along with Jesus and his disciples. In the Bible, a wedding feast is a well-known symbol of the messianic days (Isa 54:4-8; 62:4-5). The wedding and the banquet are also favorite images used elsewhere by Jesus (Matt 8:11; 9:15; 22:1-14). Abundant wine is the principal feature of such celebrations. To run short of wine on such an occasion would be a long-remembered embarrassment for any married couple. Mary takes the initiative to mention the matter to Jesus, saying, "They have no wine." Jesus responds (literally), "What is it to me and to you, woman? My hour has not yet come" (2:4).

These words of Jesus to his mother have a negative connotation. However, C.H. Giblin has shown through Johannine parallels that these words do not necessarily mean a refusal to act.[47] They mean that if Jesus does act, it will be according to *his own* purpose and design, not that of others. Therefore, at the marriage feast he will not act according to his mother's expectations but in view of his "hour." This hour will be his glorification through the cross, which will bring out his true relationship with the Father and with his people. What Jesus wants to accomplish at Cana will be evident only in the seventh and last sign on the cross. This means that the initial miracle requested by his mother is not really Jesus' ultimate purpose.

This rejection of a "wonder work" parallels the interconnected fourth sign of the multiplication of loaves. There the people misunderstand Jesus as a sign-worker and another

Moses providing miraculous bread in the wilderness. Jesus refuses to accept this understanding of his person and mission.
He withdraws to the hills away from the crowd, fearing that
they would try to make him king (6:14). In the situation of the
Johannine community, this understanding of Jesus seems to
be that of some Jewish Christians whose views of Jesus were
limited to that of Messiah and sign-worker.[48] Coming back to
Cana, the original purpose of Jesus' mother seems to reflect
this limited view. Consequently, Jesus refuses to act in this
way. Instead, he will act only in view of the coming hour on
the cross and the meaning of his death in the seventh sign.

Following Jesus' statement about his coming hour, his
mother tells the waiters, "Do whatever he tells you" (2:5). She
now acts toward the waiters (and the community) in accord
with her maternal role of remembering in the seventh sign.
She asks for perfect obedience to Jesus' word. This is noted
three times: by Mary's word, by the waiters' filling the jars
as Jesus directed, and by their obedience to his command to
bring the jars to the chief steward. We note the key parallel
to the seventh sign, where Jesus obeys the Scriptures and the
divine plan by taking the bitter wine as the cup of suffering
prepared by the Father (19:28-30). Thus Mary directs the community to obey Jesus' words, just as he has obeyed his Father's
on the cross.

What words of Jesus must they obey? In view of the interconnection between the seventh sign and the central sign of
the multiplication of loaves, the answer should be in the fourth
sign. The central crisis in this sign is the triple statement of
Jesus that his flesh must be eaten and his blood drunk (6:51-56).
How can this be possible? The seventh sign answers by showing that Jesus is indeed the new Paschal Lamb. The first sign
provides the key for believers to know how they can "con-
sume" or participate in that sacrifice. The difficult command
of Jesus can be obeyed by the believer only in the same way
as Jesus obeyed on the cross. There he accepted the "cup"
of imperfect, bitter wine, or "blood of the grape" (in Semitic

idiom) in obedience to the Father. At Cana we saw that the taking of the "cup" of good wine to the chief steward was the final act of a chain of obedience to Jesus' words. This may hint at the ritual way the believer can participate: by taking, in obedience to Jesus' word, the cup of the "blood of the grape" just as Jesus did. This emphasis on the cup is also found elsewhere. It is in Luke's account of the Last Supper, where the cup is mentioned three times in the longer Greek form of 22:17-20. It is also mentioned by Paul in 1 Corinthians 10:16 and emphasized in 1 Corinthians 10:21.

In summary, the chiastic structure of the Fourth Gospel enables us to discover the unique place of the mother of Jesus. She is present at the first and seventh signs, which explain the central sign of the loaves. At the cross, Jesus' last testament establishes the relationship of Mary and the Beloved Disciple as a continuation of his own relationship with them. This certifies the Beloved Disciple as an inner successor to Jesus and also gives special credibility to his understanding of Jesus' death as a new Passover sacrifice. Mary's role at the cross is that of a remembering mother and carrier of tradition. She is a pre-eminent witness of who Jesus is, how he died, and the effects of his death. At the first sign, the wedding feast of Cana, she instructs the community how to participate in worship in view of the meaning of Jesus' hour. She tells them to obey Jesus, just as he obeyed his Father on the cross. If they do this, they can drink a new wine of the Spirit made possible by Jesus' death on the cross.

Mary Magdalene, Apostle to the Apostles and Inner Successor of Jesus

Mary Magdalene was beside the Beloved Disciple and Jesus' mother at the cross. This suggests that she will have a special role also. Along with the others, she is a unique witness of the unusual events surrounding Jesus' death. She also, like the others, shares in their understanding of the meaning of Jesus' "hour." The presence of Jesus' mother was a guarantee for the Beloved Disciple's community in regard to succession to Jesus and authentic teaching. However, a link must also be made between this understanding of Jesus' death and the rest of the disciples, especially Peter. Here is where Mary Magdalene has the most unusual role of being the only one in John's Gospel to see the risen Jesus and bring the message of his coming ascension to the rest of the disciples.

Why was Mary Magdalene selected for this role? There is nothing about her in John's Gospel before she appears at the cross. Yet her presence there and the events following point to a special relationship between her and Jesus. We can better understand this if we first see how the Beloved Disciple in John's Gospel is not only a privileged disciple but also a model of any disciple as one whom Jesus loves.

The Disciple Whom Jesus Loved—A Model for All Those Whom Jesus Loves

"The disciple whom Jesus loved" is the favorite designation of the Beloved Disciple in the Fourth Gospel (13:23; 19:26; 20:2; 21:7, 20). This love is modeled on the reciprocal love between Jesus and his Father. This is illustrated by statements such as, "The Father loves the Son and has given all things into his hand" (see also 5:20; 10:17; 15:9). The last citation reads, "As the Father has loved me, so have I loved you; abide in my love." Therefore, the title "the disciple whom Jesus loved" represents this special love of Jesus in the relationship between himself and the above disciple. However, the expression refers not only to the Beloved Disciple but to the ideal believer as well. Thus the author refers to Lazarus in this way and also mentions that Jesus loved Martha and Mary (11:3, 5).

Mary Magdalene: Counterpart of the Beloved Disciple

The Fourth Gospel describes Mary Magdalene's relationship to Jesus in a way very similar to the way it describes the relationship between the Beloved Disciple and Jesus. She stands side by side with the Beloved Disciple and Jesus' mother during Jesus' last hour (19:25). As the Beloved Disciple becomes the inner successor of Jesus for the Johannine community, so Mary Magdalene becomes the indispensable link to "apostolic Christians"[49] under Peter's leadership. She is an apostle of apostles, the one who first sees the risen Jesus, receives a commission from him, and then notifies the others to assemble for Jesus' ascension and the gift of the Holy Spirit. All this flows from her special relationship to Jesus, which is a counterpart to that of the Beloved Disciple and Jesus.

This unique relationship is described through a detailed narration of the encounter of Mary Magdalene with the risen Jesus. Mary was so eager to visit Jesus' tomb on Easter morning that she arose while it was still dark. While Matthew, Mark, and Luke have other women accompany her, John's Gospel has only Mary Magdalene. The author wishes to single out her unusual devotion and special relationship to Jesus as a model for the true believer. Mary was completely shocked to discover that the huge circular stone at the burial entrance had been rolled aside. Fearing a grave robbery, she quickly ran to notify Peter and "the other disciple, the one whom Jesus loved." She told them, "They have taken the Lord out of the tomb, and we do not know where they have laid him" (20:2). Both men ran to the tomb to verify her statement and found that Jesus' body was missing, but they saw no signs of it being stolen; the shroud was lying on the ground, and the face covering (soudarion) was rolled up in a place by itself. No tomb robbers would have taken the time to carefully unwrap the body and leave everything so neatly.

Puzzled and dazed at not finding the body of Jesus, Mary stood outside the tomb and wept. Then she bent down to look inside the tomb again and saw two white-robed angels at the head and foot of the place where Jesus' body had been laid. They said to her, "Woman, why are you weeping?" (20:13). She replied, "Because they have taken away my Lord, and I do not know where they have laid him." Turning around, she saw a man standing there whom she thought to be the gardener, not recognizing him as Jesus. He said to her, "Woman, why are you weeping?" She said to him, "Sir, if you have carried him away, tell me where you have laid him, and I will take him away." The Gospel writer employs this threefold repetition of Mary Magdalene's words to describe her ardent longing to see the Jesus she loved so much.

"Jesus said to her, 'Mary.' She turned and said to him in Hebrew 'Rabboni!' (which means Teacher). Jesus said to her, 'Do not hold me, for I have not yet ascended to the Father; but go to my brethren and say to them, "I am ascending to my Father and your Father, to my God and your God"'" (20:16-17). Mary recognizes Jesus only when he calls her by name. Raymond Brown notes that this is a special privilege in John's Gospel.[50] As good shepherd, Jesus calls only his own sheep by name (10:3). The evangelist highlights the encounter between Mary and Jesus by noting the exact word that Mary would use in Aramaic, *Rabboni*, meaning "Master" or "Teacher." Mary Magdalene is the first person to see the risen Jesus because of her great love and strong desire to see him. In addition, Jesus gives her the unique privilege of being the first one to announce to others that he has risen from the dead.

The Old Testament background sheds special light on the meaning of the encounter between Mary and Jesus. It resembles that between a bridegroom and bride. During the Passover days the love poems of the Song of Songs were read in the synagogue. As people listened to them, they thought of God's own love for Israel. The following passage seems especially significant:

> Upon my bed by night
>   I sought him whom my soul loves;
> I sought him, but found him not;
>   I called him, but he gave no answer.
> "I will rise now and go about the city,
>   in the streets and in the squares;

I will seek him whom my soul loves.''
I sought him, but found him not.
The watchmen found me,
  as they went about in the city.
''Have you seen him whom my soul loves?''
Scarcely had I passed them,
  when I found him whom my soul loves.
I held him, and would not let him go . . . .

(Song of Songs 3:1-4)

The above text has a striking correspondence to the encounter between Mary Magdalene and Jesus in this Gospel. M. Cambe has pointed out the following details: the night atmosphere (John 20:21); the triple searching for the lover by the bride; the question addressed to the watchmen (the same word as that for ''gardener'' in Hebrew); finally, taking hold of him and not wanting to let him go.[51] Using these images, John's Gospel may be illustrating the inner meaning of the relationship between Mary and Jesus. It is like the covenant union of bridegroom and beloved in the Song of Songs.

This espousal theme is prominent in the Bible, where God's union with the people is described in nuptial terms. For example, the prophet Hosea writes: ''And I will betroth you to me for ever; I will betroth you to me in righteousness and in justice, in steadfast love, and in mercy. I will betroth you to me in faithfulness; and you shall know the Lord'' (2:19-20).

In the New Testament the Apostle Paul uses similar terminology in writing to the Corinthians about their relationship to Christ: ''I feel a divine jealousy for you, for I betrothed you to Christ to present you as a pure bride to her one husband'' (2 Cor 11:2). The Book of Revelation pictures the final stage of the kingdom of God as ''the marriage of the Lamb . . . his Bride has made herself ready'' (Rev 19:7).

By this detailed picture of Mary Magdalene's encounter with Jesus and her role as model of believers, the author presents his audience with a remarkable parallel to the intimate relationship between the Beloved Disciple and Jesus. Both are inner successors, each in a unique way, to Jesus. As with the Beloved Disciple, Mary's role is best understood in comparison with that of the other disciples, especially Peter. Only Mary risks the danger of going by herself to the tomb while it was still dark (20:1), for all followers of the crucified one must have been suspect. She is the first to notice that the tomb is empty and runs as fast as she can to tell Peter and "the other disciple, the one whom Jesus loved" (20:2). The two disciples verify that the tomb is empty, and the Beloved Disciple believes when he sees the face cloth. Peter, however, does not yet believe. Both disciples then return to the safety of home: "Then the disciples went back to their homes" (20:10).

Mary Magdalene, however, because of her overwhelming desire to find the Lord, remains by the tomb. First, angels in a vision say to her, "Woman, why are you weeping?" (20:13). Then the risen Lord, unrecognized by her, asks the same question. Finally, her persistence and faith lead to Jesus' manifesting himself to her and sending her to notify the others.

The author emphasizes the importance of Mary Magdalene's mission by noting its accomplishment: "Mary Magdalene went and said to the disciples, 'I have seen the Lord'; and she told them that he had said these things to her" (20:18). Mary Magdalene's testimony makes possible the first gathering of the disciples. Thus she has an essential role as "apostle to the apostles." In contrast, only in the final "appendix," chapter 21, does Jesus confirm Peter in the more external shepherd role by saying to him, "Feed my sheep" (21:15-17).

The term "apostle" applied to Mary Magdalene is not used in the sense of one of the Twelve. It has the special meaning of one who has seen the risen Lord and thus has special authority. This would be eminently true of the very first person to see the risen Jesus. The word "apostle" in the early Church often designated those who had this privilege. Thus Paul calls himself an apostle because he saw the risen Lord (1 Cor 15:9). In 1 Corinthians 9:1 he writes, "Am I not an apostle? Have I not seen Jesus our Lord?" The command to go tell others is similar to the command of Jesus to the Eleven at the end of Matthew's Gospel: "Go therefore and make disciples of all the nations, baptizing them in the name of the Father and of the Son and of the Holy Spirit" (Matt 28:19). Mary Magdalene's commission to "go" is more like an inner witness for others, especially the Twelve. She is really the first of all apostles in the Gospel of John. The Beloved Disciple is the first to believe on seeing the empty tomb and the face cloth, but Mary Magdalene is the first to believe as a result of the initiative of the risen Christ toward one who so ardently sought him and risked her life to be near him on the cross.

Raymond Brown has noted that the Fourth Gospel reverses another tradition that the risen Jesus first appeared to Peter and the Twelve (1 Cor 15:5; Luke 24:34).[52] The emphasis on Peter and the Twelve may be due to the need to stress external succession to Jesus and authoritative teaching. John's account may be more historical in its emphasis on a woman's witness and internal succession.

An Added Note on Martha and Mary in the Fourth Gospel

While Martha and Mary are not on the level of the mother of Jesus and Mary Magdalene, they play important roles in John's Gospel. Like Mary Magdalene, they are counterparts of the Beloved Disciple, examples of "those whom Jesus loves." We use the plural because they are portrayed as belonging to a family relationship that includes their brother Lazarus. When Lazarus became gravely ill, the two sisters sent a message to Jesus saying, "Lord, he whom you love is ill" (11:3). This phrase, "he whom you love," is the same as that designating the Beloved Disciple. The author adds, "Now Jesus loved Martha and her sister and Lazarus" (11:5) to make the family image complete. Jesus' love for Lazarus continues even after Lazarus' death, for the Jews remark at the tomb, upon seeing Jesus weeping, "See how he loved him!" (11:36).

In the story the writer gives special attention to the quality of this love. Jesus responds to the sisters' message about Lazarus' illness by saying, "Let us go into Judea again" (11:5). His disciples knew well that Jesus would risk death by going there to help Lazarus. So they answered, "Rabbi, the Jews were but now seeking to stone you, and are you going there again?" (11:8). This reply hints at a central Gospel message: Jesus will give his own life for others out of love so that they may have eternal life. In this case it is for Lazarus and his sisters. Thus Jesus practices his own words, "Greater love has no one than this, that a person lay down life itself for friends" (15:13).

Martha responds to Jesus' love by a great act of faith in him, despite the human impossibility of his promise to raise Lazarus. Jesus said to her, "Do you believe this?" She answered, "Yes, Lord; I believe that you are the Christ, the Son of God, he who is coming into the world" (11:27). In this confession of faith Martha represents the faith of the Johannine community. Her confession parallels that of Peter in Matthew's Gospel (16:16). It is a deep inner and personal response that will be illustrated in the anointing at Bethany.

We have already seen that Luke transformed this anointing in accord with the purposes of his Gospel. John's Gospel, like those of Matthew and Mark, has the story before the passion, but the author skillfully retells it in view of his own teaching concerns. Here once again we are not trying to delve into sources or find out what originally may have happened or uncover various layers of editorship. We presume that the Gospel in its final form was written in narrative drama, with a special message to the audience that they could understand.

> Six days before the Passover, Jesus came to Bethany, where Lazarus was, whom Jesus had raised from the dead. There they made him a supper; Martha served, and Lazarus was one of those at table with him. Mary took a pound of costly ointment of pure nard and anointed the feet of Jesus and wiped his feet with her hair; and the house was filled with the fragrance of the ointment (12:1-3).

The atmosphere of the story suggests a family reception for Jesus before the Passover and his death. Martha fulfills her family role by serving at table, as in Luke's story (Luke 10:38-42). Mary in turn welcomes the important guest by the customary washing of feet. However, it is done in a way that can only result from extraordinary devotion and love. This is shown in two ways: first, by the extremely expensive ointment, a symbol of Mary's own self-giving; second, by letting down her hair and wiping his feet. Anne Winsor has shown that this action is a special symbol of love in the light of feminist exegesis of the text.[53]

The phrase "the house was filled with the fragrance of the ointment" (12:3) symbolizes the far-reaching effects of this family reception of Jesus. It echoes the words of the prologue, "To all who received him, who believed in his name, he gave power to become children of God" (1:12). This loving reception of Jesus is reciprocated by Jesus at his final supper. There he washes the disciples' feet in response to Mary's action. This washing is a final act of reception and hospitality to welcome the disciples into the heavenly home to which he is returning.[54] This is brought out also by the introduction to the story: "Jesus knew that the hour had come to depart out of this world to the Father" (13:1).

By way of conclusion, the Fourth Gospel has presented a unique portrait of key women in order to bring out its central message. This Gospel, unlike the others, is a journey of the eternal Logos into the world and its return to the Creator. The journey of the earthly Jesus, by way of comparison, is like an external journey in which the inner Logos is at work. Therefore, the hero of the drama is the Logos, for whom there can be no counterpart.

However, the inner successor of Jesus, the incarnate Logos, is the *Paraklētos*, or Holy Spirit, who remains with the disciples forever. The principal embodiment of this Spirit is the Beloved Disciple of Jesus and source of the Fourth Gospel. The guarantee of his place as an inner successor to Jesus comes from his close association with the Master, and especially from Jesus' last testament on the cross. Here the mother of Jesus becomes supremely important. She continues with the Beloved Disciple the relationship of mother and son that was the privilege of herself and Jesus. As a witness of Jesus' death and as a remembering mother, she also guarantees the unique understanding of Jesus' death as a new Passover that is brought out in this Gospel. Thus she could be called a "hidden hero" in this sense. The role is "hidden" because it is enclosed within an understanding of the mysterious interconnecting signs of the Fourth Gospel, especially the first and the last.

Mary Magdalene also has a unique role as a counterpart of the Beloved Disciple and supreme example of "one whom Jesus loves." With Jesus' mother and the Beloved Disciple she is also a witness of the meaning of Jesus' death. In John's Gospel she is the *only one* to see the risen Lord and to bring the message of his coming ascension to the remaining disciples, who have gathered together to await the Master's appearance. Thus she deserves the unique title of "apostle to the apostles."

A Final Reflection

Our study has shown that each of the Gospels has presented a portrait of a counterpart of Jesus in accord with its particular purposes. This hero is usually hidden within the dramatic and literary structure of each document. This person is not merely an ideal or example for the audience; instead, *she is a necessary part without which the Gospel could not have been written.* In Matthew, Mark, and Luke, without Mary Magdalene and the other women there would have been no witnesses to Jesus' death, burial, empty tomb, and resurrection. Hence Jesus would have died alone, and the story would have ended there. In John's Gospel, Jesus' mother is the guarantee that the Beloved Disciple, source of the Gospel, is a genuine successor to Jesus and that his understanding of Jesus' death and mission is trustworthy. In the same Gospel, Mary Magdalene performs an essential role as apostle to the apostles. She is the only link between the risen Jesus and the disciples who gather together after she announces to them that she has seen Jesus.

Consequently, Christianity, like the beginnings of the human race, owes its origins to the cooperation between a man and woman: a hero Jesus and his counterpart, each of whom was necessary to the other. The Fourth Gospel tells us that the Holy Spirit is to continue on and duplicate the work of Jesus. Therefore the signs of the presence of this Spirit are those that characterized its origins. Only the free and equal cooperation of man and woman within communities of believers can be an adequate sign of the presence of that Spirit.

NOTES

Publication data for books and articles mentioned in the following Notes may be found in the Bibliography, page 141.

1. Among the scholars who have dealt with the Gospels as dramatic narratives are G. Bilezekian, A. Culpepper, W. Kelber, J. D. Kingsbury, D. Rhoads and D. Michie, V. Robbins, R. Tannehill, and T. Weeden.

2. This can mean that women's roles may have been deliberately hidden within the Gospels so that they would be more appealing to such an audience. W. Munro's study, *Women Disciples in Mark*, is especially valuable in this regard.

3. This helpful distinction has been increasingly utilized in Gospel studies, for example in the work of D. Rhoads and J. D. Kingsbury.

4. The division and texts have been taken from the research of Van Iersel.

5. Valuable information on the nature of this persecution and the Gospel response can be found in D. Senior, "With Swords and Clubs." See also S. G. F. Brandon, "The Date of the Markan Gospel."

6. D. Rhoads and D. Michie, *Mark as Story*, p. 3.

7. *Jesus the Teacher: A Socio-Rhetorical Interpretation of Mark.*

8. The significance of Jesus' central question, "Who do you say I am?" for the whole Gospel of Mark has been brought out by H. Fledderman, *The Central Question of Mark's Gospel.*

9. See D. Senior, "With Swords and Clubs."

10. The selections below are taken from S. Johnson, *The Gospel According to St. Mark*, p. 256.

11. Here we have drawn from the study of F. Matera, *The Death of Jesus According to Luke*, pp. 473–474.

12. This sequence has been illustrated by H. L. Chronis, "The Torn Veil."

13. Chronis, "The Torn Veil," p. 110.

14. *Ibid.*

15. From S. Johnson, "Greek and Roman Heroes."

16. M. Hengel, *The Atonement*, p. 32.

17. E. Fiorenza, *In Memory of Her*, p. xiii.

18. M. Lagrange, *Evangile selon Saint Marc*, p. 367.

19. E. Fiorenza, *In Memory of Her*, p. xiii.

20. This total mission orientation of Mark as seen by modern scholars has been surveyed by D. Senior in "The Struggle to Be Universal."

21. This has been brought out by C. R. Catchpole, "The Fearful Silence of the Women at the Tomb."

22. This view has been advanced by C. Boomershine and G. L. Bartholomew, "Narrative Technique of Mark 16:8."

23. See W. D. Davies, *The Setting of the Sermon on the Mount*.

24. J. D. Kingsbury, *Matthew as Story*.

25. D. Senior, "The Death of Jesus and the Resurrection of the Holy Ones," p. 325.

26. T. L. Donaldson, *Jesus on the Mountain*, shows how the mountains in the Gospel of Matthew serve as a literary and rhetorical narrative device.

27. A detailed enumeration of texts that bring out the Jesus/Moses parallel are found in R. H. Gundry's literary study of the Gospel of Matthew entitled *Matthew: A Commentary on His Literary and Theological Art*. After examining these it is hard to agree with Donaldson that the mountains in Matthew do not bring out this theme.

28. A comparative study of the narratives of feeding the crowds in the four Gospels brings out Matthew's focus on Jesus' person in his account. For details, see J. Grassi, *Loaves and Fishes*.

29. In the Bible, service to the poor and hungry was regarded as direct obedience to God's commands. The same viewpoint seems likely in regard to Jesus' final commands to feed the hungry, give drink to the thirsty, etc. See J. Grassi, "I Was Hungry and You Gave Me to Eat."

30. The Hellenistic world, like much of the ancient world, was very conscious of energy patterns and communication in what they considered a live universe. Jesus' words and the gospel message would be interpreted as real forces at work in the world. See J. Nolland, "Grace as Power."

31. R. H. Gundry, *Matthew: A Commentary on His Literary and Theological Art*, p. 173. His detailed literary study of Matthew's text has been very valuable in discovering the special work of the evangelist in the passages we are studying.

32. An example of the fruitful study of the Gospel and Acts as a unified theology is that of R. F. O'Toole, *The Unity of Luke's Theology*.

33. J. Plevnik's study "The Eyewitnesses of the Risen Jesus in Luke 24" shows that Luke has oriented his whole narrative toward emphasizing the place of Peter and the Twelve.

34. The special purpose of Luke in combating Gnostic tendencies has been brought out by C. H. Talbert, *Luke and the Gnostics*, especially in regard to this passage.

35. This title and its basis in Luke is found in the excellent study of J. Neyrey, *The Passion According to Luke*, pp. 140–142.

36. In a survey of the biblical background of *dikaios*, F. Matera, "The Death of Jesus According to Luke," has found that the primary meaning of *dikaios* in this passage is that of the "just one" in terms of fulfilling God's scriptural plan. However, the theme of innocence is also contained in this scriptural picture of the "just one." This has been studied in detail by D. Schmidt.

37. For the Lukan theme of Jesus as judge, see J. Neyrey, *The Passion According to Luke*, pp. 121–126.

38. See J. Kilgallen, "John the Baptist, the Sinful Woman and the Pharisee."

39. A much more detailed presentation of Mary as mother and model of believers is found in J. Grassi, *Mary, Mother and Disciple*.

40. This meaning, along with its literary sources, has been proposed by E. Cole.

41. The first-century Jewish historian Josephus praises Sarah as the most beautiful of all women (*Antiquities*, I.8.1). The Genesis Apocryphon of the Dead Sea Scrolls (chap. XX) has a long praise of her beauty.

42. M. DeGoedt, "Un schème de révélation dans le quatrième evangile," illustrates this by comparison with similar Johannine texts.

43. R. E. Brown, *The Community of the Beloved Disciple*, p. 197.

44. In an article explaining the sign structure of the Fourth Gospel, "La composition structurelle des sept signes dans le quatrième evangile."

45. R. E. Brown in his *Gospel According to John*, vol. I, pp. 527–530.

46. J. M. Ford has illustrated this from Jewish law and literary texts.
47. C. H. Giblin has shown this through parallels in other Johannine texts.
48. R. E. Brown, *The Community of the Beloved Disciple*, p. 169, has described one of the groups addressed by the Gospel in this manner but has not connected it to this text.
49. R. E. Brown, *The Community of the Beloved Disciple*, pp. 165–170, has described them as Christians under Peter's leadership who had a moderately high Christology but did not yet understand the Johannine teachings of Jesus' pre-existence.
50. R. E. Brown, "Roles of Women in the Fourth Gospel," p. 694.
51. M. Cambe, "L'influence du Cantique des Cantiques sur le Nouveau Testament."
52. R. E. Brown, "Roles of Women in the Fourth Gospel," p. 692.
53. In an unpublished paper on the anointing at Bethany in John 12:1-8.
54. H. Weiss has shown that the washing of the disciples' feet by Jesus should be understood in terms of the traditional reception of a guest into a home.

BIBLIOGRAPHY OF WORKS CITED

Bilezekian, G. *The Liberated Gospel: A Comparison of the Gospel of Mark and Greek Tragedy*. Grand Rapids, Mich.: Baker, 1977.

Boomershine, C., and G. L. Bartholomew. "Narrative Technique of Mark 16:8." *Journal of Biblical Literature* 100:213–223.

Brandon, S.G.F. "The Date of the Markan Gospel." *New Testament Studies* 7 (1961) 126–141.

Brown, R. E. *The Gospel According to John*. Garden City, N.Y.: Doubleday, 1966.

———. *The Community of the Beloved Disciple*. New York: Doubleday, 1979.

———. "Roles of Women in the Fourth Gospel." *Theological Studies* 36 (1975) 688–699.

Cambe, M. "L'Influence du Cantique des Cantiques sur le Nouveau Testament." *Revue Thomiste* 62 (1962) 5–26.

Catchpole, D. R. "The Fearful Silence of the Women at the Tomb. A Study of Markan Theology." *Journal of Theology of South Africa* 18 (1977) 3–10.

Chronis, H. L. "The Torn Veil: Cultus and Christology in Mark 15:37-39." *Journal of Biblical Literature* 101 (1982) 97–114.

Cole, E. "What Did Luke Mean by *Kecharitōmenē?*" *American Ecclesiastical Review* 139 (1958) 228–239.

Culpepper, R. A. *Anatomy of the Fourth Gospel: A Study in Literary Design*. Philadelphia: Fortress, 1983.

Davies, W. D. *The Setting of the Sermon on the Mount*. Cambridge: Cambridge University Press, 1964.

DeGoedt, M. "Un schème de révélation dans le quatrième evangile." *Novum Testamentum* 8 (1962) 142–150.

Donaldson, T. L. *Jesus on the Mountain: A Study in Matthean Theology*. *Journal for the Study of the New Testament*, Supplement 8. Sheffield: *Journal for the Study of the Old Testament* (1985).

Ellis, P. *The Genius of John: A Composition-critical Commentary on the Fourth Gospel*. Collegeville, Minn.: The Liturgical Press, 1984.

Fiorenza, E. *In Memory of Her*. New York: Crossroads, 1983.

Fledderman, H. "The Central Question of Mark's Gospel: A Study of Mark 8:29." Doctoral diss., Graduate Theological Union, San Francisco, 1978.

Ford, J. M. " 'Mingled Blood' from the Side of Christ (John xix. 34)" *New Testament Studies* 15 (1968–69) 337–338.

Giblin, C. "Suggestion, Negative Response, and Positive Action in St. John's Portrayal of Jesus." *New Testament Studies* 26 (1980) 197–211.

Girard, M. "La composition structurelle des sept signes dans le quatrième évangile." *Sciences Religieuses* 9 (1980) 315–324.

Grassi, J. " 'I Was Hungry and You Gave Me to Eat': The Divine Identification Ethic in Matthew." *Biblical Theology Bulletin* 11 (1981) 81–84.

_____. *Loaves and Fishes: The Gospel Feeding Narratives*. Wilmington, Del.: Michael Glazier (forthcoming).

_____. *Mary, Mother and Disciple*. Wilmington, Del.: Michael Glazier, 1988.

_____. "The Role of Jesus' Mother in John's Gospel: A New Approach." *Catholic Biblical Quarterly* 48 (1986) 67–80.

Gundry, R. H. *Matthew: A Commentary on His Literary and Theological Art*. Grand Rapids, Mich.: Eerdmans, 1982. References to the Jesus-Moses theme are found in the topical index.

Hengel, M. *The Atonement: The Origins of the Doctrine in the New Testament*. Philadelphia: Fortress, 1981.

Johnson, S. *The Gospel According to St. Mark*. New York: Harper, 1960.

_____. "Greek and Jewish Heroes: Fourth Maccabees and the Gospel of Mark." In *Early Christian Literature and the Classical Intellectual Tradition in Honorem Robert M. Grant*, edited by W. Schoedel and R. Wilken, 155–176. Paris: Editions Beauchesne, 1979.

Kelber, W. *Mark's Story of Jesus*. Philadelphia: Fortress, 1979.

Kilgallen, J. "John the Baptist, the Sinful Woman and the Pharisee." *Journal of Biblical Literature* 104 (1986) 675–679.

Kingsbury, J. D. *Matthew as Story*. Philadelphia: Fortress, 1986.

Lagrange, M. *Evangile selon Saint Marc*. Paris: J. Gabalda, 1947.

Matera, F. "The Death of Jesus According to Luke: A Question of Sources." *Catholic Biblical Quarterly* 47 (1985) 473–474.

Minear, P. "The Beloved Disciple in the Gospel of John: Some Clues and Conjectures." *New Testament Studies* 19 (1977) 105–123.

Munro, W. "Women Disciples in Mark." *Catholic Biblical Quarterly* 44 (1982) 225–241.

Neyrey, J. *The Passion According to Luke*. New York: Paulist, 1985.

Nolland, J. "Grace as Power." *Novum Testamentum* 28 (1986) 26–31.

O'Toole, R. F. *The Unity of Luke's Theology*. Wilmington, Del.: M. Glazier, 1984.

Plevnik, J. "The Eyewitnesses of the Risen Jesus in Luke 24." *Catholic Biblical Quarterly* 49 (1987) 90–103.

Rhoads, D. "Narrative Criticism and the Gospel of Mark." *Journal of the American Academy of Religion* 50 (1982) 411–434.

_____ and D. Michie. *Mark as Story: An Introduction to the Narrative of a Gospel*. Philadelphia: Fortress, 1982.

Robbins, V. *Jesus the Teacher: A Socio-Rhetorical Intrepretation of Mark*. Philadelphia: Fortress, 1984.

Schmidt, D. "Luke's 'Innocent Jesus': A Scriptural Apologetic." In *Political Issues in Luke-Acts*, edited by R. J. Cassidy and P. J. Scharper. Maryknoll, N.Y.: Orbis, 1983.

Senior, D. " 'With Swords and Clubs'—Mark's Critique of Abusive Power," *Biblical Theology Bulletin* 17 (1987) 10–20.

_____. "The Struggle to Be Universal: Mission as a Vantage Point for New Testament Investigation." *Catholic Biblical Quarterly* 46 (1984) 63–81. Senior has a bibliographical discussion of other authors who have presented this viewpoint, especially in regard to Mark.

_____. "The Death of Jesus and the Resurrection of the Holy Ones (Mt 27:51-53)." *Catholic Biblical Quarterly* 38 (1976) 312–329.

Smith, R. H. "Darkness at Noon: Mark's Passion Narrative." *Concordia Theological Monthly* 44 (1973) 325–338.

Talbert, C. H. *Luke and the Gnostics*. Nashville: Abingdon, 1966.

Tannehill, R. "The Disciples in Mark: The Function of a Narrative Role." *Journal of Religion* 57 (1977) 386–405.

Van Iersel, B. "The Gospel of St. Mark—Written for a Persecuted Community." *Nederlands Theologisch Tijdschrift* 34 (1980) 15–36.

Weeden, T. *Mark—Traditions in Conflict*. Philadelphia: Fortress, 1971.

Weiss, H. "Footwashing in the Johannine Community." *Novum Testamentum* 21 (1979) 298–325.